非物质文化遗产在广西
Intangible Cultural Heritage in Guangxi
중국 광시의 무형문화유산

中英韩对照
Chinese-English-Korean Edition

译著：**孟繁旭　诸慧琴**

本书系桂林理工大学科研成果
广西哲学社会科学规划项目"广西'壮族三月三'文化外译与国际传播研究"（编号：21BYY003）阶段成果

前　　言

广西是多民族聚居的自治区，世居少数民族有壮、瑶、苗等11个，其中壮族是广西也是中国人口最多的少数民族，这些居住在广西的少数民族在历史的发展中不断积累了宝贵的文化财富，有记录壮族始祖布洛陀创世神话的民间文学，有"壮族三月三"、"瑶族盘王节"、"京族哈节"、"壮族蚂拐节"等充满少数民族特色的节日，也有"壮族织锦技艺"、"侗族木构建筑营造技艺"等凝聚少数民族智慧的传统技艺。

广西的各族人民在日常的生产生活中总是喜欢以歌叙事，以歌抒情，有曲调婉转的侗族大歌，犹如天籁的瑶族蝴蝶歌，以及独具特色的壮族三声部，还有一批极具地方风韵的传统戏剧，如桂剧、广西文场、桂林渔鼓等……这些都是广西的文化名片，也是广西的国家级非物质文化遗产。

本书选取37个有代表性的广西国家级非遗项目，使用中、英、韩三语对照的方式向读者概述广西的非遗文化，同时每个非遗名录都配有插画，图文并茂的形式将37项广西国家级非物质文化遗产逐一生动呈现。希望本书能帮你开启探索广西之旅，感受壮美广西的魅力。

Preface

Guangxi is a multi-ethnic autonomous region with 11 ethnic groups, such as Zhuang, Yao and Miao, among which Zhuang is the most populous ethnic group in Guangxi and China. These ethnic groups living in Guangxi have accumulated precious cultural wealth in the course of historical development. These wealth includes folk literature recording the creation myth of Buluotuo, the ancestor of Zhuang, festivals full of ethnic characteristics such as "March the 3rd festival of Zhuang", " Panwang festival of Yao", "Hafestival of Jing" as well as "Maguai Festival of Zhuang", as well as traditional craftsmanship with ethnic wisdom including "Craftsmanship of Zhuang Brocade" and "Architectural craftsmanship for timber-framed structures of Dong".

People of all ethnic groups in Guangxi prefer to express themselves and communicate with each other in the form of songs in their daily life and work. Typical examples include the melodious grand song of Dong, ethereal butterfly song of Yao and the unique three-part folk songs of Zhuang. There are also a number of traditional operas with local charm, such as Gui opera, Guangxi Wenchang, Guilin Yugu Tunes, etc.. All the examples above are the national intangible cultural heritage of Guangxi, which are considered as the cultural name cards of Guangxi.

In this book, 37 representative Guangxi national intangible cultural heritage items are selected and introduced to readers in three languages, including Chinese, English and Korean. At the same time, each item is illustrated with vivid pictures. We hope this book could provide a guide for your exploring journey to Guangxi and a window for you to find the charm of Guangxi ethnic culture.

目录：
CONTENTS

第一编　民间文学
Series 1 Folk Literature

1. 布洛陀 The Epic of Buluotuo　　　　　　　　　　>> 5
2. 刘三姐歌谣 Liu Sanjie Ballad　　　　　　　　　　>> 13
3. 壮族嘹歌 Liao Song of Zhuang Ethnic Group　　　>> 21
4. 密洛陀 Miluotuo　　　　　　　　　　　　　　　　>> 29
5. 壮族百鸟衣故事 The Story of Hundred-Bird-Coat　>> 35

第二编　民间音乐
Series 2 Folk Music

6. 侗族大歌 Grand Song of the Dong Ethnic Group　　　　　>> 40
7. 那坡壮族民歌 Napo Folk Song of Zhuang Ethnic Group　　>> 46
8. 瑶族蝴蝶歌 Butterfly Song of Yao Ethnic Group　　　　　>> 53
9. 壮族三声部 Three-part Folk Song of Zhuang Ethnic Group　>> 58
10. 广西八音 Guangxi Bayin music　　　　　　　　　　　　　>> 64
11. 京族艺术 Single-stringed Fiddle ArZZt of Jing Ethnic Group　>> 70

第三编　传统舞蹈
Series 3 Traditional Dance

12. 田林瑶族铜鼓舞 Tianlin Bronze Drum Dance of Yao Ethnic Group　>> 76
13. 瑶族长鼓舞 Long Drum Dance of Yao Ethnic Group　>> 83
14. 藤县狮舞 Lion Dance of Teng County　　　　　　　>> 89

15. 田阳壮族狮舞 Lion Dance of Tianyang Zhuang Ethnic Group　　>> 95
16. 铜鼓舞（南丹勤泽格拉）Bronze Drum Dance(Chinzegra)　　>> 101
17. 瑶族金锣舞 Jinluo Dance of Yao Ethnic Group　　>> 106

第四编　民俗
Series 4 Folk Custom

18. 京族哈节 Ha Festival of Jing Ethnic Group　　>> 113
19. 毛南族肥套 Feitao of Maonan Ethnic Group　　>> 120
20. 瑶族盘王节 Panwang Festival of Yao Ethnic Group　　>> 126
21. 壮族歌圩 Song Fair of Zhuang Ethnic Group　　>> 132
22. 壮族蚂拐节 Maguai Festival of Zhuang Ethnic Group　　>> 140
23. 壮族铜鼓习俗 The bronze drum custom of the Zhuang Ethnic Group　　>> 147
24. 宾阳炮龙节 Firecracker Dragon Festival in Binyang　　>> 152
25. 龙胜瑶族服饰 Costumes of Longsheng Yao Ethnic Group　　>> 158
26. 钦州跳岭头 Tiao Lingtou in Qinzhou　　>> 164
27. 壮族霜降节 Frost's Descent Festival of Zhuang Ethnic Group　　>> 170
28. 壮族三月三 March 3rd Festival of Zhuang Ethnic Group　　>> 177
29. 中元节（资源河灯节）Ziyuan River Latern Festival　　>> 186

第五编　传统戏剧、曲艺及传统技艺
Series 5 Traditional Opera and Craftsmanship

30. 桂剧 Gui Opera　　>> 191
31. 桂南采茶戏 Guinan(South of Guangxi) Tea-picking Opera　　>> 199
32. 壮族七十二巫调音乐 Zhuang Witch Songs with Seventy-two Tunes　　>> 205
33. 广西文场 Guangxi Wenchang　　>> 212
34. 桂林渔鼓 Guilin Yugu Tunes　　>> 219
35. 侗族木构建筑营造技艺 Architectural craftsmanship for timber-framed structures of Dong Ethnic Group　　>> 227
36. 壮族织锦技艺 Craftsmanship of Zhuang Brocade　　>> 233
37. 钦州坭兴陶 Qinzhou Nixing pottery　　>> 241

非物质文化遗产在广西
Intangible Cultural Heritage in Guangxi
중국 광시의 무형문화유산

에듀컨텐츠·휴피아
CH Educontents·Huepia

1. 布洛陀

The Epic of Buluotuo

[入选时间：2006 Time: 2006

遗产名录：第一批国家级非物质文化遗产名录

Heritage Category: The First Batch of National Intangible Cultural Heritage

地域：百色   Region: Baise]

《布洛陀》是壮族的长篇诗体创世神话，主要记述了壮民族的"祖公"布洛陀开天辟地、创造人类的丰功伟绩。在壮族语言发音中，"布"是很有威望的老人的尊称，"洛"是知道、知晓的意思，"陀"是很多、很会创造的意思，"布洛陀"就是一个知道很多、很会创造的老人。布洛陀是壮族先民根据自己对生活的认识、按照自己的理想和愿望，把自己的一切智慧、知识、气魄，都集中地概括在他身上，使之成为寄托理想、人人拥戴、个个崇拜的民族祖先神。

The epic of Buluotuo is a long poetic myth of creation of the Zhuang ethnic group. It mainly tells the story of the remarkable achievements of the Zhuang ancestor god, Buluotuo, who is the genesis and creation of man. In Zhuang language, "Bu" is a respectable word for venerable elder man, "luo" means knowing and "tuo" refers to being able to create. Based on their own understanding of life, ideals and wishes, Zhuang ancestors concentrated all their wisdom, knowledge and courage on Buluotuo, making him an ideal national ancestor god welcomed and worshiped by everyone.

『포락타』는 쫭족의 장편 창세사시로 주로 쫭족의 '조공'인 포락타가 천지개벽을 하여 인류를 창조한 위대한 업적을 기술하고 있다. '포'는 매우 유망이 있는 노인의 존칭이며, '락'는 안다의 의미며 '타'는 매우 잘 창조한다는 뜻이다. '포락타'는 많이 알고, 창조를 잘하는 노인을 말한다. 포락타는 쫭족 선민들이 자신들의 생활에 근거하고 자신들의 기대와 희망에 따라 모든 지혜, 지식, 기백을 그에게 집약하여 기탁하고 사람마다 받들고 숭배하는 민족의 조상신이 되었다.

在很长的一段历史时期，布洛陀史诗只是口头传唱，大约在明代，出现了古壮文手抄本，开始以书面的形式保存下来。古壮文手抄本《布洛陀史诗》长达万行，分四个部分，共十九章：第一部分是开头歌，分为礼歌、问答歌、石蛋歌；第二部分是创造歌，分为初造天地、造人、造太阳、造火、造谷米、造牛；第三部分是治理歌，分为再造天地、分姓；第四部分是嘱咐歌。整部史诗的内容可以归纳为布洛陀创造天地、造人、造万物、造土皇帝、造文字历书和造伦理道德六个方面，以诗歌的语言和形式叙述了天地日月的形成、人类的起源、农作物的栽培、牲畜的饲养以及壮族先民氏族部落社会的情况。整部史诗结构宏伟、格调庄重、艺术想象丰富、浪漫色彩浓厚，运用了大量的比拟、夸张、复叠等表现手法。

In a long period of history, *the Epic of Buluotuo* was only passed on orally. Around Ming Dynasty, manuscripts of ancient Zhuang scripts appeared and was preserved in the written form. The manuscripts of *the Epic of Buluotuo* in ancient Zhuang scripts, as long as ten thousand lines, were divided into four parts, totaling nineteen chapters: the first part was the opening song, which was divided into ritual song, question and answer song and stone egg song; the second part was the creation song, which is divided into the first creation of heaven and earth, man, sun, fire, millet rice and cattle; the third part was the governance song, which is divided into the rebuilding of heaven and earth, and the division of surnames; the fourth part was exhortation song. The content of the whole epic could be summarized into six aspects, namely, creation of heaven and earth, creation of human beings, creation of universe, creation of emperors, creation of character and almanac, and creation of ethics and morals. In the language and form of poetry, it tells the stories of the formation of heaven and earth, the origin of human beings, the plantation of crops, the domestication of livestock, as well as the situation of the clan and tribal society of the ancestors of the Zhuang ethnic group. The whole epic has the features of magnificent structure, solemn style, rich artistic imagination and strong romantic color. It uses a large number of expression techniques such as comparison, exaggeration and duplication.

아주 오랜 역사시기에 포락타 사시는 구두로 전해지다가 대략 명조때에 고장문 필사본이 출현하면서 서면형식으로 보존되기 시작하였다. 고장문(古莊文) 필사본 「포락타 서사시」는 1만 행으로 4개 부분, 총 19장으로 되어 있다. 제1 부분은 서두 노래로, 예가, 문답가, 석단노래로 나뉜다. 제2부분은 창조의 노래로, 천지 만들기, 사람 만들기, 태양 만들기, 불 만들기, 쌀 만들기, 소 만들기로 나눈다. 제3부분은 다스림 노래로, 천지를 재건하고 성을 나눈다. 제4부분은 당부가이다. 전체 서사시는 천지창조, 인간, 만물, 황제, 문자와 역사서, 윤리를 만드는 등

6개 내용으로 귀납할 수 있다. 시가의 형식으로 천지 일월의 형성, 인류의 기원, 농작물의 재배, 가축의 사육과 장족 선민 씨족 부락 사회의 상황을 서술하고 있다. 전반 서사시는 구조가 웅대하고 격조가 장중하며 예술적 상상력이 풍부하고 낭만적 색채가 짙으며 대량의 비유, 과장, 반복 등의 표현수법을 사용하였다.

作为壮族一部古老而又内容丰富的创世史诗，布洛陀史诗主要流传于广弭红水河流域、右江流域及左江流域的广大壮族地区，云贵南、北盘江流域的壮语和布依语地区亦有流传。同时布洛陀文化还波及东南亚的泰国、缅甸、老挝、越南等国家和地区，成为促进中国与东盟国家保持友好经贸往来的重要组成部分，也是中国东盟一带一路建设的重要组成部分。

As an ancient and rich creation epic of Zhuang ethnic group, *the Epic of Buluotuo* is mainly prevailing in the vast Zhuang-populated areas of Guangmi Hongshui river basin, Youjiang and Zuojiang river basin as well as the Zhuang language and Buyi language areas south and north of Panjiang river basin in Yunnan and Guizhou provinces. At the same time, Buluotuo culture is also spread to Thiland, Myanmar, Laos, Vietnam and other countries and regions in Southeast Asia, and has become an important part of maintaining economic and trade exchanges between China-ASEAN, as well as the important part of the construction of China-ASEAN One Belt One Road.

쫭족의 오래되고 내용이 풍부한 창세 서사시로서 포락타 시는 주로 광부홍수하 유역, 우강 유역 및 좌강 유역의 광대한 쫭족 지역에서 유전되었으며 운남과 귀주의 남쪽, 베이반장 유역의 쫭어(壯語)와 포이어(布依語) 지역에서도 전해졌다. 동시에 포락타 문화는 동남아의 태국, 미얀마, 라오스, 베트남 등 국가와 지역에 파급되어 중국과 아세안 국가의 우호적인 경제 무역 거래를 촉진하는 중요한 구성 부분일 뿐만 아니라 중국 아세안 일대일로 건설의 중요한 구성 부분이기도 하다.

广西田阳县敢壮山被认定是布洛陀文化的发祥地，由于人们对布洛陀的虔诚崇奉，这里便成为人们朝拜、祭祀始祖布洛陀，寄托情思的文化圣地。由于朝拜和祭祀活动的延续，这里也成为传承布洛陀创世史诗、传播布洛陀文化的场所。每年的农历三月初七到初九，海内外几十万壮族同胞都会自发来到布洛陀起源的敢壮山，祭祀始祖布洛陀。

Ganzhuang Mountain in Tianyang County, Guangxi is regarded as the birthplace of Buluotuo culture and a cultural holy land for people to worship and offer sacrifices to the ancestor god Buluotuo. Due to the continuation of the worship activities, it has also become a place to inherit the creation epic of Buluotuo and spread Buluotuo culture. Every year from the seventh day to the ninth day of the third lunar month in China, hundreds of thousands of Zhuang people from home and abroad will spontaneously come to Ganzhuang Mountain to offer sacrifices to the ancestor god, Buluotuo.

광시 티안양현 용장산은 포락타문화의 발상지로 인정받았다. 사람들이 포락타를 경건하게 숭배함으로 인해 이곳은 사람들이 시조인 포락타에게 참배하고 제사를 지내 감정을 기탁하는 문화 성지가 되었다. 순례와 제사가 계속되면서 이곳은 또한 포락타 창세 서사시와 포락타 문화를 전파하는 장소가 되었다. 매년 음력 3월 7일부터 9일이면 국내외 몇 십만 명의 쫭족동포들이 자발적으로 포락타가 기원한 용장산에 와서 포락타에게 제사를 지낸다.

布洛陀创世史诗和歌颂布洛陀创世业绩歌谣，可以说是壮族先民的一部原生形态的百科全书，其中保存着壮族先民对客观世界、对自然环境的幼稚认识，保存着壮族先民与自然作斗争的历史，凝聚着壮族先民千百年来在生产、生活等方面积累下来的智慧和经验，在历史学、文学、宗教学、古文字学、音韵学和音乐学研究等方面具有一定的学术价值。

Buluotuo creation epic and the ballads praising Buluotuo's creation achievements can be considered to be an encyclopedia of the primitive form of Zhuang ancestors, which preserves their naïve understanding of the objective world and natural environment, the history of struggling with nature, embodies the wisdom and experience gained by Zhuang ancestors over thousands of years in production and life, and provides academic value for the study on history, literature, religion, ancient philology, phonology and musicology.

在广西，刘三姐歌谣家喻户晓，流传于广西各壮族聚居地区。刘三姐被广西民间视为"歌仙"，明清以来，有关她的传说与歌谣文献记载很多。广西宜州市是刘三姐歌谣最有代表性的地区，被认为是刘三姐的故乡。

Liu Sanjie Ballad is well-known and spread in various Zhuang-populated communities in Guangxi. Liu Sanjie is regarded as a "song fairy" by Guangxi folk. Since the Ming and Qing Dynasties, there have been many legends and ballads about her in literature. Yizhou is the most representative place of *Liu Sanjie Ballads* and is considered to be her hometown.

유삼저가요는 광서에서 모두가 다 알고 있으며 광서 여러 쫭족 집거지역에서 전해지고 있다. 유삼저(刘三姐)는 광시(廣西) 민간에서 '가선(歌仙)'으로 간주되는데, 명·청(明·淸) 이래로 그녀와 관련된 전설과 가요 문헌에 많은 기록이 있다. 광서 의주시는 유삼저가요가 가장 대표적인 지역으로 유삼저의 고향으로 꼽힌다.

桂西宜山地区有关刘三姐的传说讲述的是，刘三姐出生在在宜山下枧河边中枧村，从小聪明伶俐，有着出口成歌的本领，被认为是黄莺投胎。远近的青年与三姐对歌，没有一个能比过她。财主莫仁怀，见三姐貌美善歌，就想纳其为妾。找来三名广东水客与三姐对歌，但都被三姐打败。莫仁怀就处处刁难，最后砍断葡萄藤，使三姐坠入河中。三姐飘至柳州，在柳州鲤鱼峰对歌，连唱三天三夜，飘然逸去。之后又在桂林七星岩对歌，连唱七天七夜，变为一对黄莺飞去。宜州地区的刘三姐传说随着岭西与周边地区的交流，不断扩大，目前已经成为中国南方最著名的区域性传说之一。

In Yishan regions of Guixi (West of Guangxi) the legendary about Liu Sanjie tells a story about a girl surnamed as Liu in the Zhongjian Village on the lower Jian River at the foot of Yishan Mountain. Sanjie was so clever and capable to make songs spontaneously that she was regarded as the incarnation of a lark. Young men near and afar came to sing to her and no one could equal her. Coveting her beauty and talent, a local tyrant named Mo Huairen from Mo Village wanted to take Sanjie as his concubine. He sent three fishermen to challenge Sanjie but they were defeated by her, which infuriated Mo. He plotted to murder Sanjie and finally cut the grape vine to causing her fall into the river. Sanjie was floated in the river to the city of Liuzhou, where she had duet singing on the Carp Peak for three successive days and nights. Then she appeared in Seven Star Cave in Guilin, where she sang for seven days and nights and eventually turned into a pair of larks. The legend of Liu Sanjie in Yizhou area has expanded with the communication between Guangxi and the surrounding areas, and has become one of the most famous regional legends in southern China.

계림 서쪽에 위치한 이산(宜山) 지역의 유삼저에 관한 전설에 따르면, 유삼저는 이산 하견(下枧) 중견 마을에서 태어났으며 어릴 때부터 총명하고 노래를 부르는 재주가 있어 꾀꼬리의 환생으로 여겼다. 먼 곳의 청년들이 유삼저와 노래를 겨루는데 누구도 그녀를 견줄 만한 사람이 없었다. 부자 막인회(莫仁怀)는 유삼저의 미모와 노래 솜씨를 보고 첩으로

맞으려고 3명의 광동 수객을 불러 유삼저와 노래를 겨루었지만 모두 유삼저에게 패했다. 막인회는 도처에서 괴롭히다가 나중에는 포도덩굴을 잘라 유삼저를 물에 빠뜨렸다. 유삼저는 류주에 가서 류주의 잉어봉에서 노래를 겨루며 연속 사흘 밤낮을 노래하고는 유유히 사라졌다. 그리고 계림 칠성암에서 노래를 겨루었다. 7일 밤낮 노래를 불렀더니 한 쌍의 꾀꼬리가 되어 날아갔다. 의주 지역의 유삼저 전설은 영서지역과 주변지역 간의 교류와 더불어 끊임없이 확대되어, 지금은 이미 중국 남방의 가장 유명한 지역전설의 하나로 되었다.

从地域文化角度看，刘三姐传说虽然在广东乃至湖南、云南、贵州的苗、瑶、布依、仫佬、汉等民族中都有同类的故事流传，但广西无可厚非地被认为是刘三姐传说的发源地，也是其传播、流传的中心。深受群众熟悉、喜爱的歌舞剧《刘三姐》以及同名电影都取材于这一传说。2004年3月由张艺谋总导演的大型山水实景剧 《印象·刘三姐》 在桂林阳朔开始公演，以现代流行音乐的形式 重新演绎了 "藤缠树" "蝶恋花" "多谢了" 等多首脍炙人口的刘三姐歌谣。 目前刘三姐已经成为广西的文化品牌。

(图片来于网络)

From the regional cultural perspective, though there are similar folk stories of Liu Sanjie spreading in Han group as well as the ethnic groups of Miao, Yao, Buyi, Mulao in Guangdong, Hunan, Yunnan and Guizhou provinces, Guangxi is undoubtedly considered as the birthplace of Liu Sanjie legend as well as its prevailing center. The Drama "Liu Sanjie" and the Movie "Liu Sanjie", which are well-known and loved by the public are based on this legend. In March 2004, "Impression Liu Sanjie", a large-scale landscape drama directed by Zhang Yimou, was performed in Yangshuo, Guilin. It re-interpreted many popular ballads of Liu Sanjie in the form of modern pop music, such as "The tree is wrapped around the vine", "The butterfly loves the flower" and "Heartfelt thanks". At present Liu Sanjie has become a cultural brand of Guangxi.

지역문화의 측면에서 볼 때, 비록 유삼저 전설은 광동, 후난, 윈난, 구이저우의 먀오, 요오, 부이, 무라기, 한 등 민족들에게서도 비슷한 이야기가 전해지고 있지만 광시는 유삼저 전설의 발원지이자 전파의 중심이라고 볼 수 있다. 대중들에게 널리 알려지고 사랑받는 가무극 「유산저」와 동명 영화도 모두 이 전설에서 소재를 얻었다. 2004년 3월, 장이모(張藝謀)가 총 연출한 대형 산수실 경극 〈인상·유삼저〉가 계림 양쉬에서 공연을 시작하였다. 현대 대중음악의 형식으로 〈등나무 휘감기〉, 〈접연화〉, 〈고맙습니다〉 등 많은 유명한 유삼저 가요를 리메이크하였다. 현재 유삼저는 이미 광시의 문화 브랜드가 되었다.

刘三姐歌谣内容广泛, 包括天文地理、神话传说、岁时农事、日常生活、伦理道德、恋爱婚姻等各个方面。按题材分, 大体分为生活歌、生产歌、爱情歌、仪式歌、谜语歌、故事歌及创世古歌七大类。刘三姐歌谣中, 情歌的数量最多, 艺术水平也最高。这些歌谣具有以歌代言的诗性特点和鲜明的民族性, 传承比较完整, 歌谣种类丰富多样, 且传播广泛。

Liu Sanjie Ballad covers a wide range of subjects, including astronomy, geography, mythology, farming, daily life, ethics, love and marriage. In terms of theme, it is generally divided into seven categories, namely, life songs, production songs, love songs, ritual songs, riddle songs, story songs and ancient creation songs. Among these ballads, love songs rank the first in both number and artistic level. With the features of poetic expression through singing and distinctive ethnicity, these ballads are completely inherited and spread in rich varieties and forms.

유삼저 가요의 내용은 천문·지리·신화와 전설·세시 농사·일상생활·윤리·도덕·연애·혼인 등 여러 방면을 포괄한다. 소재에 따라 크게 생활가, 생산가, 사랑가, 의식가, 수수께끼가, 이야기노래 및 창세고가의 일곱 가지로 나눈다. 유삼저의 가요 중에서 사랑노래가 수량이 가장 많고 예술수준도 가장 높다. 이런 가요는 노래로 대변되는 시적 특징과 선명한 민족성을 갖고 있고 비교적 완전하게 전승되었으며 종류가 풍부하고 다양할 뿐만 아니라 널리 전파되었다.

刘三姐歌谣作为壮族人民精神生活的产物，已成为壮族之魂，在全国乃至全世界都产生了深远的影响，显示了中华民族民间传统艺术活态文化的魅力。它不仅具有文化史研究价值，还具有民族学、人类学、社会学、美学等方面的研究价值。

As a product of the spiritual life of Zhuang people, *Liu Sanjie ballad* has become the soul of the Zhuang people and has exerted a profound influence around China and the world, showing the charm of living cultures in Chinese traditional folk arts. It possess research values not only in the field of cultural history but also in Ethnology, Anthropology, Sociology, Aesthetics and so on.

유삼저가요는 쫭족 인민의 정신생활의 산물로서 이미 쫭족의 혼이 되었고 전국 나아가서는 전 세계에 심원한 영향을 끼쳤으며 중화민족 민간전통 예술과 활기찬 문화의 매력을 보여 주었다. 그것은 문화사 연구가치 뿐만 아니라, 민족학, 인류학, 사회학, 미학 방면의 연구 가치도 가지고 있다.

3. 壮族嘹歌

Liao Song of Zhuang Ethnic Group
[入选时间：2008   Time: 2008
遗产名录：第二批国家级非物质文化遗产名录
Heritage Category: The Second Batch of National Intangible Cultural Heritage
地域：百色   Region: Baise]

壮族嘹歌是著名的壮族长篇古歌，是经过长期的口头传诵后，由壮族文人的加工和删改，用古壮字记录并在格式上作了适当规范的歌谣集。主要流行于广西壮族自治区右江中游的平果、田东、田阳县和红水河流域的马山县、大化瑶族自治县以及属邕江流域的武鸣县境内。

Liao Song of Zhuang Ethnic Group is the famous long ancient song of Zhuang. After a long time of oral circulation, it has become a songbook which was readjusted by Zhuang scholars and was recorded in ancient Zhuang characters. It is mainly popular in the following counties of Guangxi, namely, Pingguo, Tiandong, and Tianyang in the middle reaches of Youjiang River, Mashan county and Dahua Yao Autonomous county in Hongshui river basin, and Wuming county in Yongjiang river basin.

좡족료가는 유명한 장편고대노래로서 장기간 구두로 전해지다가 좡족문인들이 가공하고 삭제, 수정하여 고장으로 기록하고 형식을 적당히 규범화한 가요집이다. 광시좡족자치구 유강 중류의 핑궈, 톈둥, 톈양현과 훙수이허 유역의 마산현, 다화야오족자치현 및 옹강 유역의 우밍현에서 주로 유행한다.

壮族嘹歌是因为其唱法中每一句都有"嘹—嘹—嘹"作为衬词拖腔而得名。在壮语中，"嘹"含有"唱歌玩乐"的意思，是壮族"好歌""以歌为乐"的民族文化心理的生动体现。因此，壮族嘹歌之名源于壮族"以歌为乐"、好唱"嘹嘹（辽辽）之歌"的习俗。壮族嘹歌不只是某个历史时期的作品，而是壮族古代民歌发展到一定阶段的产物。晋代《交州记》中就有壮族先民"乘牛唱辽辽之歌"的记载。今壮族地区许多民歌演唱都有"辽罗""辽辽罗""辽啦""啦辽啦"等衬词,这"辽辽之歌"就是壮族嘹歌形成的基础。从壮族嘹歌所反映的内容看,其最后形成的时间是在明代。当时,随着治所在今平果县境内的思恩府的社会文化的发展,出现了一批兼通壮汉文化的壮族文人,他们用古壮字把流传在民间的壮族嘹歌记录整理起来,并进行了一定的删改、加工和规范,使之得以以口头和书写两种方式传播。

Liao Song of Zhuang gained its name for the modal words of "Liao-Liao-Liao" in the drawl of each singing lines. In Zhuang Language, "Liao" has the meaning of "singing and enjoying" and it is also the embodiment of Zhuang people's national cultural psychology, "loving songs" and "singing for fun". Therefore, the name of *Liao Songs of Zhuang* comes from Zhuang people's custom of "singing for fun" and "love singing Liao Liao songs". *Liao Songs of Zhuang* are not only a work of certain historical period but also a product of the development of Zhuang people's ancient folk songs. It has been recorded in *Jiaozhou Record* of Jin Dynasty that Zhuang people's ancestors sang Liao Liao songs while riding cows. Nowadays, many folk songs in Zhuang regions have the modal words of "liao luo", "liao liao luo", "liao la", "la liao la". These Liao Liao songs are the foundation of *Liao Songs of Zhuang*. Judging from its contents, *Liao Songs of Zhuang* came into final being in Ming Dynasty. At that time, with the development of

Si Enfu's(name of local government in Ming) social culture of the administrative center in nowadays Pingguo County, a group of Zhuang literati who are also good at Han culture recorded the folk *Liao Songs of Zhuang* in ancient Zhuang characters after improvements, which contributed to the circulation of *Liao Song of Zhuang ethnic group* in terms of both oral and written forms.

쫭족료가는 창법에서 매 구절마다 모두 '료-료-료'라는 부조로 사용되기 때문에 명명된 것이다. 쫭족 담화에서 '랴오닝'에는 '노래하고 즐기다'라는 뜻이 들어 있는데, 이는 '좋은 노래'와 '노래를 즐거움으로 삼다'는 쫭족의 민족 문화 심리를 생동감 있게 보여 주는 것이다. 료료라는 이름은 "노래를 즐거움으로 삼아", "료료(랴오요)의 노래"를 부르기 좋아하는 쫭족의 풍습에서 유래되었다. 쫭족료가는 어느 한 역사시기의 작품일 뿐만 아니라 쫭족의 고대민요가 일정한 단계로 발전한 산물이다. 진(晉) 나라 「교주기(交州記)」에는 쫭족 선민이 "소를 타고 요나라의 노래를 불렀다"는 기록이 있다. 현재 쫭족 지역의 많은 민요에는 모두 "료오", "료료오", "료라", "라료라" 등과 같은 부사가 있는데, 이 "료의 노래"는 쫭족 소리가 형성된 기초이다. 쫭족료가의 내용을 보면 가장 최종적으로 형성된 시간은 명조이다. 당시 사회 문화가 발전함에 따라 쫭족과 한족 문화를 모두 아는 문인들이 많이 모였는데 그들은 고대 한 글자로 민간에 떠도는 쫭족 노래를 기록하고 정리하기 시작하였으며 일정 한 수정, 가공과 규범화하면서 구두와 서면 두 가지 방식으로 전파되었다.

壯族嘹歌的内容相对固, 是反映壯族人民劳动、生产、生活、爱情、婚姻、历史等方面内容的传统民歌。根据广西平果县歌手唱歌和抄歌的习惯，壮族嘹歌分为《日歌》《夜歌》《散歌》三大部分，共有4000多首，16万多行。《日歌》又分为两套长歌和三个短歌；《夜歌》由三套长歌和六个短歌组成；《散歌》是各种生活的写照，如《十年天旱歌》讲的是灾情，《丰收歌》讲的是风调雨顺、向往太平生活，《二十四季节歌》讲的是农事活动等。

Liao songs of Zhuang has a relatively fixed content. As a traditional folk song it reflects the labor, production, life, love, marriage, history and other aspects of Zhuang people. According to the singing and copying habits of singers in Pingguo County, Guangxi, *Liao Song of Zhuang* is divided into three categories: *Day song*, *Night song* and *Causal song*, with a total number of more than 4000 pieces and 160,000 lines. *Day song* contains two sets of long songs and three short songs, while *Night song* is composed of three sets of long songs and six short songs. *Casual song* is related with daily life, such as *Ten years Draught Song* about disasters, *Harvest song* about peace and smooth life, and *Twenty-Four-Solar -Term song* about agricultural activities.

쫭족료가의 내용은 상대적으로 견고하며 쫭족 인민의 노동, 생산, 생활, 사랑, 혼인, 역사 등 방면의 내용을 반영한 전통 민요이다. 광서 평과현의 가수들이 노래하고 노래를 베껴 부르는 습관에 근거하여 쫭족료가는 ≪일가≫, ≪야가≫, ≪산가≫ 등 3개 부분으로 나뉘는데 총 4,000여곡,

16만여줄로 되어 있다. ≪해가≫는 2조의 장가와 3조의 단가로 나뉘며 ≪밤의 노래≫는 3조의 장가와 6조의 단가로 구성되었고「散歌」는 각종 생활의 묘사로, 예를 들면「십년천가노래」는 재해를 말하고,「풍작노래」는 날씨가 좋고 태평한 생활을 동경하는 것을 말하고,「이십사계절절이」는 농사 활동을 말한다.

《三月歌》是壮族嘹歌的重要长歌，主要描写初春时节，壮家青年结伴来到青山旁、泉水边、树荫下、花丛中，采鲜花、摘嫩笋、拾蕨菜的欢乐景象。当人们流连忘返之际，春雨喜降，雨水入田，紧张繁忙的春耕季节来到了，人们纷纷赶回家中，修农具、运肥料、犁田地、播种育秧。紧张的劳动，更激起人们歌唱的热情，他们边春耕、边唱歌，一直唱到第二年的正月十五。

March song is an important long song of *Liao Song of Zhuang ethnic group*, which mainly describes the following scenes: in early spring season Zhuang youth gathered with peers to pick flowers, bamboo shoots and ferns in the places of green mountains, spring side, tree shades, and flower beds; while enjoying themselves, spring rain fell into the field, signifying the start of the busy farming season; people rushed back home to repair farming tools, transport fertilizer, plow the field and plant seedlings; people's enthusiasm for singing has been aroused by the tense labor and they sang while working until the 15th day of the first lunar month next year.

「삼월가」는 좡족료가의 중요한 장가로 주로 초봄 무렵 좡족 집안의 청년들이 동반하여 청산옆, 샘터, 나무그늘 아래, 꽃밭에 와서 꽃을 따고 어린 죽순을 따고 고사리를 줍는 즐거운 광경을 묘사한다. 사람들이 집에 돌아가는 것을 잊고 있을 때, 봄비가 반갑게 내려 빗물이 논으로 들어가고 바쁜 봄갈이철이 온다. 사람들은 집으로 서둘러 돌아가, 농기구를 수리하고, 비료를 운반하고, 밭을 갈고, 파종을 하고 모를 기른다. 긴장한 노동으로 사람들은 노래에 대한 열정을 더욱 불러일으켰다. 그들은 봄갈이를 하면서 이듬해 정월 보름까지 노래를 불렀다.

壮族嘹歌是原生态民歌，已经深深地影响到壮族的每一个人，每一个家庭以及他们的社会生活的多个方面，甚至还影响到壮民族文化的传承和社会的进步发展等等，在文学、历史学、民俗学、古文字研究等方面都有重要的研究价值。

Liao song of Zhuang ethnic group is an original ecological folk song, which has deeply influenced every Zhuang people, every Zhuang family and many aspects of their social life, and even influenced the inheritance of Zhuang ethnic culture and the social progress and development. They also have important research value in many fields including Literature, History, Folklore, and Ancient Chinese Character.

좡족료가는 토착 민가가 있을 뿐만 아니라, 좡족의 모든 사람, 가정 및 사회생활 등 모든 측면에서 깊은 영향을 미치고 있다. 심지어 좡족 민족

《密洛陀》是流传于广西都安、巴马等地瑶族聚居区的神话古歌,布努瑶族第二大支系的一首创世古歌,千百年来传唱不断,深受广大瑶族人民喜爱。"密洛陀"是布努瑶交际语词,"密"意为"母亲","洛陀"意为"古老",两者合起来即为"古老的母亲"。由于瑶族历史上只有本民族语言,没有本民族文字,这首古老的歌谣便依靠瑶族人民口口相传,世代流传,而"密洛陀"也早已人名化,指古代造天造地造万物造人类的那位女神。

Miluotuo is a mythic ancient song popular in Du'an, Bama and other areas inhabited by the Yao ethnic group in Guangxi. As an ancient creation song of the second largest branch of the Bunu Yao ethnic group, it is handed down through recitation and singing over the centuries, and deeply loved by the mass of Yao ethnic group. Miluotuo is a communicative words of Bunu Yao and is a combination of "mi" and "luotuo", in which the former means "mother" and the later means "ancient". Since there was no written characters but ethnic language in the history of Yao ethnic group, this ancient ballad was handed down orally from generation to generation. Miluotuo has become a name, referring to the ancient goddess who created the world.

「밀낙타」는 광시의 도안(都安), 바마(巴马) 등지의 요족(瑶族) 밀집지역에 전해지는 신화 옛노래이다. 부누(布努) 요족의 제2대 분계의 창세 옛노래로

수천 년 동안 불려왔고 많은 요족 사람들의 사랑을 받았다. "밀낙타"는 부누요의 사교어로, "밀낙타"는 "어머니"를 뜻하고 "낙타"는 "오래됨"을 뜻하며, 둘을 합치면 "오래된 어머니"가 된다. 요족 역사상 민족의 언어만 있고 민족의 문자는 없었기 때문에 이 고대 가요는 요족 사람들에게 구전, 대대로 전해져 왔다. 또한 "밀낙타"는 고대에 하늘과 땅을 창조하고 만물을 창조하고 인류를 창조한 여신을 뜻하여 이미 유명해졌다.

《密洛陀》以浩瀚的篇幅,通过形象生动的诗的语言,讲述了密洛陀的诞生、天地日月的形成、人类万物的起源、治理大地山河、征服自然灾害、和妖魔怪兽的斗争、族性分开继宗接代、密洛陀续寿及病故、族内外的矛盾和冲突、本族迁徙的原因和经过等重大事件,热烈地歌颂了布努瑶始祖母密洛陀的伟大业绩。

Recorded by vast length and vivid language of the poem, Miluotuo tells the story of many important events and great achievements of Bunu Yao ancient foremother, Miluotuo, including the birth of Miluotuo, the formation of the Sun and Moon, the origin of both human and things, governance of the earth, mountain and rivers, conquer of natural disasters, battle with monsters and demons, separation of caste and succession of generation, the prolonged living and death of Miluotuo, conflicts in and out of groups, reasons and process of group migration.

밀낙타 넓은 편폭으로, 형상을 통하여 생동한 시적 언어로 부처님의 탄생, 천지 일월의 만물의 기원, 형성, 인간이 다스리는 대지와 산천, 자연재해, 요괴 괴물과의 투쟁, 민족 분열과 계승, 밀낙타의 장수와 병사, 민족 내외의 갈등과 충돌, 본향 이동의 원인과 경위 등 중대한 사건을 서술하고 있으며, 부누요의 조상인 밀낙타의 위대한 업적을 열렬히 노래하였다.

传说在农历五月二十九日，布洛西山和密洛陀山两座神山忽然各进出一个人来，女的是密洛陀，男的是布洛西，两人结成夫妻，成为布努瑶的始祖。因此，每年的五月二十九日，布努瑶人都要过"达努节"来祭祀他们的祖神密洛陀。"达努"在瑶语中是"永不忘"的意思，蕴含了不忘密洛陀创始功绩的意思。"达努节"又被叫作"祖娘节"、"二九节"、"祝著节"和"瑶年"。在达努节上，族人们会聚在一起跳节日中最神圣的乐舞—铜鼓舞，铜鼓舞鼓声铿锵雄浑，舞姿粗犷剽悍，非常感人。入夜后，人们还会跳起代表瑶民生活的兴郎铁玖舞，一直舞到深夜，最后会在老人们集体对唱的"密洛陀"颂歌中结束。

As the legend goes, on the 29th day of the fifth lunar month, the woman named Miluotuo and the man named Buluoxi suddenly came out from the sacred Mount Miluotuo and Buluoxi respectively. They got married and became the forefathers of Bunu Yao. Therefore, every year on this day, Bunu Yao people will celebrate "Danu Festival" to offer sacrifice to their ancient goddess Miluotuo. In Yao language," Danu" means "never forget", which contains the meaning of never forgetting the foundation achievements of Miluotuo. "Danu Festival" also called "Foremother Festival", "Two Nine Festival", "Wishing Festival" and Yao Year". On Danu Festival, group people will get together to have the most sacred musical dance, Bronze Drum Dance which is touching with vigorous clanging and bold posture. When the night comes, people will also have the dance named "Xing lang tie jiu" (a dance represents the life of Yao people) until late night. Finally they will end up in the chorus of "Miluotuo" sung by the old people.

전설에 의하면, 음력 5월 29일에 포나서산과 밀낙타산이라는 두 산에서 갑자기 한 사람씩 나타났는데 여자는 밀낙타이고 남자는 포나시였다. 이 두 사람은 부부가 되어 부누요의 시조가 되었다. 매년 5월 29일, 부누요 사람들은 "다누 축제"를 통해 조상인 밀낙타에게 제사를 지낸다. 다누는 요어로 영원히 잊지 않는다는 뜻으로 밀낙타의 업적을 잊지 않는다는 뜻을 담고 있다. 다누절은 조모의 날, 29절, 축저절과 요년이라고도 한다. 다누절에 사람들은 한데 모여 명절에서 가장 성스러운 악무인 동고춤을 추는데 동고춤은 소리가 낭랑하고 힘차며 춤모습이 호방하고 용감하여 사람들을 감동시킨다. 밤이 되면 요민의 생활을 상징하는 흥랑철구(興郎鐵九) 춤을 심야까지 추다가 노인들이 함께 부르는 '밀낙타'를 시작으로 막을 내린다.

《密洛陀》是一部集布努瑶的历史、地理、风俗、信仰、民约于一体, 熔布努瑶神话、传说、故事、歌谣、寓言为一炉的百科经典。在历史学、宗教学、文化艺术学和少数民族语言等学科有重要的学术价值,同时《密洛陀》也是一部传授布努瑶生产斗争知识、生存斗争知识和生活习俗的古老教科书。

Miluotuo is a collection of the history, geography, folklores, beliefs and convents of Bunu Yao people, as well as a classic encyclopedia of myth, legends, story, song and fable of Bunu Yao. It is of great academic value in the fields of history, religion, culture, art and ethnic languages. At the same time, Miluotuo is also an ancient textbook which covers Bunu Yao's knowledge of production, survival and life customs.

「밀낙타」는 부누요의 역사, 지리, 풍속, 신앙, 민약을 하나로 융합하고 부누요의 신화, 전설, 이야기, 가요, 우화를 하나로 융합한 백과경전이다. 역사학, 종교학, 문화예술학, 소수민족언어 등 학과에서 중요한 학술적 가치가 있으며, 〈밀낙타〉는 또한 부누요의 생산 투쟁지식, 생존 투쟁지식과 생활 풍습을 전수한 오래된 교과서이기도 하다.

5. 壮族百鸟衣故事

The Story of Hundred-Bird-Coat
[入选时间：2014　Time: 2014
遗产名录：第四批国家级非物质文化遗产名录
Heritage Category: The Fourth Batch of National Intangible Cultural Heritage
地域：南宁　Region: Nanning]

"百鸟衣"故事是流传于广西横县校椅一带的壮族民间传说故事,富有幻想性的神话色彩,其流传随着历史的发展而不断丰富。故事讲述了在远古的"土司"统治时期贫苦农民古卡和其妻子依娌的故事,土司因贪恋依娌的美貌而将其抢走。临走时依娌嘱咐古卡制弓箭,射一百只鸟,用羽毛制成神衣,一百天后穿着百鸟衣到州府相会。古卡历尽艰辛,制成百鸟衣后,按时来到州府。古卡借献衣之机杀死了土司,夫妻俩双双把家还。

The story of *Hundred-Bird Coat* is a folk tale of Zhuang ethnic group popular in the area of XiaoYi Town Hengxian County Guangxi. It is full of fantasy and mythic color and constantly enriched by the historical development. As the story goes, during the reign of the Chieftain in ancient times, a poor peasant named Guka had a beautiful wife names Yili who was taken away by the Chieftain for her beauty. Before leaving Yili asked Gukato to make bows and arrows, shoot a hundred birds to make a coat with the feathers, and come to the state government with the coat to meet her. Guka did as Yili told and they killed the chieftain while offering the coat. They returned home happily in the end.

'백조의의 이야기'는 광시 헝셴(衡县) 일대에 전해지는 쫭족 민간전설로 환상적인 신화색채가 풍부하다. 역사의 발전과 더불어 그 전승은 끊임없이 풍부해지고 있다. 이 이야기는 고대의 토쓰(土司) 통치시대에 가난한 농부 쿠카와 그의 아내 이리의 이야기를 다루고 있다. 토쓰는 이리의 미모에 반하여 그를 빼앗아간다. 떠날 때 이리는 쿠카에게 활과 화살을 만들어 새

100 마리를 잡아 깃털로 신의를 만들어 100일 후에 백조옷을 입고 주정부에 가서 만나자고 하였다. 쿠카는 갖은 고생을 거쳐 백조옷을 만든 후 그 시간에 주정부로 왔다. 쿠카는 옷을 바치는 기회를 빌어 토쓰를 죽이고 부부는 함께 집으로 돌아갔다.

广西壮族著名作家韦麒麟根据当地流传的"百鸟衣"故事创作了叙事长诗《百鸟衣》，该作品的出现将壮族文学带入了中国的文坛，还被翻译成英、法、意、日等十三个国家的文字，在国外广为传颂，也向世界展示了中国少数民族文学的迷人风采。在该作品的影响下，出现了大量以"百鸟衣"为题材而创作编演的邕剧、粤剧、壮剧和歌舞剧等，广西电影制片厂还根据"百鸟衣"的故事拍摄了电影《百鸟衣》。

Wei Qilin, a famous Zhuang writer, created a narrative poem "Hundred-Bird-Coat", which brought Zhuang Literature into China's literary world. The work has been translated in 13 languages, including English, French, Italy and Japanese. Known overseas, the work also presented the charm of China's ethnic literature to the world. Under its influence, a great number of operas with *Hundred-Bird-Coat* theme have been edited and performed, including Yong Opera, Yue Opera, Zhuang Opera and Musical Dance Opera. The film of *Hundred-Bird-Coat* was produced by Guangxi Film Company based on the same story.

6. 侗族大歌

Grand Song of the Dong Ethnic Group

[入选时间：2006　Time: 2006

遗产名录：第一批国家级非物质文化遗产名录

Heritage Category: The First Batch of National Intangible Cultural Heritage

地域：柳州　Region: Liuzhou]

侗族是中国少数民族中的一员，至今已有2500多年的历史，主要聚居在中国贵州、湖南、广西、湖北。广西的侗族大歌流传于广西柳州市三江侗族自治县沿溶江河一带的侗寨。侗族村寨大多依山傍水，风光秀美。侗族人都能歌善唱，他们聚集的村寨随时都会飘起动人的歌声。男耕女织的淳朴生活使他们的歌声更加纯净，贴近自然。

Dong is one of China's ethnic minorities, boasting a history of more than 2,500 years, and mainly inhabited in Guizhou province, Hunan province, Guangxi province and Hubei province. The Grand Song of the Dong Ethnic Group of Guangxi is circulated in the Dong villages along Rongjiang River in Sanjiang Dong Autonomous county of Guangxi. Most Dong villages have beautiful sceneries surrounded by mountains and lakes, which are filled with the beautiful singing of their people. The rich mixture of the singing talent of Dong people and the simple, rustic life they live makes their singing sound purer and closer to life.

동족은 중국의 소수민족 중 하나로, 지금까지 2500년 이상의 역사를 가지고 있으며, 주로 구이저우(貴州), 후난(湖南), 광시(广西), 후베이(湖北)에 모여 살고 있다. 광서의 동족노래는 광서 류주시 삼강동족자치현 연용강하 일대의 동마을에서 전해졌다. 동족마을은 대부분 산을 등지고 물을 가까이하고 풍경이 수려하다. 동족 사람들은 모두 노래를 잘 부르는데 그들이 모인 마을에서는 수시로 사람을 감동시키는 노랫소리가 울린다. 남자들이 농사짓고 여자들이 옷감을 짜는 순박한 생활은 그들의 노랫소리를 더욱 순수하고 자연과 가깝게 만들었다.

侗族大歌历史久远,早在宋代就已经发展得比较成熟。大歌是侗族人民集体歌唱的多声部民歌,一般在村寨或氏族之间集体做客的场合中演唱,是侗族人文化交流和情感交流的核心内容。

With a long history, the Grand Song of the Dong ethnic group had been continuously developing and maturing since the Song Dynasty. It is a multiple-part folk song and usually sung on the occasions when people from different villages or clans gather together. It is a key means of cultural and affective interactions among the Dong people.

동족대가는 역사가 유구한바 송나라때 이미 비교적 성숙된 발전을 가져왔다. 대가는 동족이 단체로 부르는 다성부 민요로, 일반적으로 마을이나 씨족 사이에서 단체로 부르는 장소에서 부르게 되며, 동족의 문화 교류와 감정 교류의 핵심 내용이다.

侗族大歌种类繁多,可分为声音歌、叙事歌、童声歌、踩堂歌、拦路歌等,内容主要是歌唱自然、劳动、爱情和友谊。大歌曲式结构独特,每首歌均由"歌头"、"歌身"和"歌尾"三部分组成,通常为二声部,由三人以上进行演唱,讲究押韵,曲调优美。歌唱者模拟鸟叫虫鸣、高山流水等自然界的声音,充满了原生态的气息。

The Grand Song of Dong ethnic group is rich in variety, can be classified into acoustic songs, narrative songs, *Caitang* songs and *Lanlu* Songs by style and into those about nature, work, love or friendship by content. The grand songs are characterized by a unique structure, each composed three parts," the beginning", " the body" ,and "the end", and being usually a two-part song sung by three or more people in a carefully tailored rhyme and a beautiful melody. The singers imitate sounds such as those of birds, insects, mountains and rivers, filling the sounds with a natural flavor.

동족대가요는 소리노래·서사노래·아동노래·당밟기노래·길막이노래 등으로 종류가 많고, 내용은 주로 자연·노동·사랑·우정을 노래한다. 대가곡형식의 구조는 독특하다. 매 곡은 모두 "노래 머리", "노래 몸"과 "노래 끝"의 세 부분으로 이루어지며 보통 2성부로 3명 이상이 노래를 진행하며 압운에 주의를 기울이며 곡조가 아름답다. 성악가들이 새 울음소리, 벌레 울음소리, 높은 산과 흐르는 물 등 자연의 소리를 흉내내어, 원시적인 분위기가 물씬 풍긴다.

和许多古老的民族一样，侗族没有自己的民族文字。侗族大歌以独特的形式承载传递了这个民族的生活方式、社会结构、人伦礼俗、历史智慧等至关重要的文化信息。侗族人认为歌就是知识，就是文化，谁掌握的歌多，谁就是有知识的人。因此在侗族地区，歌师受到尊重和爱戴，被认为是最有知识、最懂得道理的人。

Like many other ancient ethnic groups, the Dong ethnic group doesn't have its own written language. The Grand Song, as a unique means, has carried and passed down the way of life, social structure, human relations and customs, historical wisdom and other vital cultural information of the Dong ethnic group. It is believed by the Dong people that songs are knowledge and culture, and that a knowledgeable person is the one who masters a number of songs. Therefore, in Dong-populated area, masters of Grand Song are highly respected and esteemed, being considered as the most intelligent and reasonable people.

옛날의 많은 민족들과 마찬가지로 동족도 자체의 민족문자가 없다. 동족대가는 독특한 형식으로 이 민족의 생활양식, 사회구조, 인륜, 예절, 역사적 지혜 등 중요한 문화정보를 담고 있다. 동족들은 노래는 곧 지식이고 문화이며 노래를 많이 소유하는 사람이 곧 유식하다고 여긴다. 이 때문에 동족 지역에서 노래하는 사원은 가장 박식하고 사리를 잘 아는 사람으로 존중과 사랑을 받고 있다.

每当重大节日来临，或者是有集体交往活动，或是远方来了尊贵的客人，侗族人就会登上村寨标志性建筑——鼓楼放声高歌。魅力的侗族村寨，一时成了歌的海洋。侗族大歌不仅是一种音乐艺术，而且是侗族社会结构、婚恋关系、文化传承和精神生活的重要组成部分。它曲目众多，内容极为广泛，具有社会史、婚姻史、思想史、教育史等多方面的研究价值，是维系侗族社会生存的精神支柱。

Whenever there is an important festival, a group activity, or a distinguished guest coming from afar, the Dong people will climb up the drum tower, the landmark of their village, to sing the songs to their hearts' content, turning the beautiful village into a sea of music. The Grand Song of Dong ethnic group is not only a kind of musical art but also an important component of Dong group's social structure, marriage and love relations, cultural inheritance and spiritual life. Rich in number and content, it possess research value in many fields related with the study of history, such as society history, marriage history, thinking history and education history. It is a spiritual pillar maintaining the continuation of the Dong society.

매번 중대한 명절이 다가오거나 단체교류활동이 있거나 멀리서 귀한 손님이 오면 동족사람들은 마을의 표식건축인 고루에 올라가 큰소리로 노래를 부른다. 매력적인 동족 마을은 일순간 노래의 바다로 변했다. 동족대가는 음악예술일 뿐만 아니라 동족의 사회구조, 결혼, 연애관계, 문화전승과 정신생활의 중요한 구성부분이다.곡목이 많고 내용이 광범하며 사회사, 혼인사, 사상사, 교육사 등 다방면에서 연구 가치가 있고 동족의 사회생존을 유지하는 정신적 기둥이다.

7. 那坡壮族民歌

Napo Folk Song of Zhuang Ethnic Group

[入选时间：2006　Time: 2006

遗产名录：第一批国家级非物质文化遗产名录
Heritage Category: The First Batch of National Intangible Cultural Heritage

地域：百色　Region: Baise]

那坡壮族也称"黑衣壮",是壮族中具有奇特色彩的一个族群,自称"敏"、"仲"、"嗷",因着装全黑而得名,主要聚居在位于中越边境的广西那坡县。

Napo Zhuang, also known as "Heiyizhuang", is a unique ethnic group among the Zhuang people. They call themselves "Min", "Zhong", "Ouch", and they are named for their all-black clothes. Napo Zhuang mainly inhabited in Napo County of Guangxi, which locates on the border with Vietnam.

검은 옷차림 (黑義莊) 이라고도 하는 나포좡족은 좡족 중 특이한 색채를 지닌 민족으로 자칭 민 (民), 중 (仲), 으 (으) 이라고 한다. 옷을 모두 검은색으로 입었다고 해서 붙여진 이름이다. 중국과 베트남 국경지대에 있는 광시 (廣西) 나포현에 주로 모여 살고 있다.

那坡县的黑衣壮人不仅能歌,还很善舞,从三岁的小孩子到古稀的老人都能够伴着古乐翩翩起舞。黑衣壮人至今仍保存着古朴完整、多姿多彩的民间歌谣,被誉为"广西民族音乐富矿"和壮族民歌的"活化石"。

Heiyizhuang people in Napo are good at both singing and dancing. No matter what age people in Napo are able to dance with the ancient music. Heiyizhuang still preserves ancient, complete and colorful folk songs, and is known as the "rich mine of Guangxi national music" and the "living fossil" of Zhuang folk songs.

나파현의 흑의장(黑의상) 사람들은 노래를 잘할 뿐만아니라 춤도 잘 추는데 3살 어린아이로부터 고희의 로인에 이르기까지 모두 옛날 음악에 맞춰 춤을 추었다. 헤이의쫭족은 고풍스럽고 완전하며 다채로운 민간가요를 보존하고 있어 '광시 민족 음악의 부광'과 쫭족 민요의 '살아 있는 화석'으로 불린다.

那坡壮族民歌来源于其民族的生产劳动, 日常生活, 节庆活动等, 极富生活情趣。在内容上, 那坡壮族民歌主要有神话传说、人物传记、环境变迁、历史事件等的叙事歌; 倾吐苦难、控诉压迫的苦情歌; 反映自然、生活经历的农事歌; 向往美景的赞颂歌; 接人待物的礼仪歌; 表现传统习惯的风俗歌; 吊唁奔丧的祭祀歌; 庆祝婚嫁满月、新居落成、老人生日的祝酒歌, 以及内容丰富的情歌。

Napo folk songs of Zhuang are derived from their national production and labor, daily life and festival activities, which are full of life interest. The songs mainly include the following contents: narrative songs of myths and legends, biographies of characters, stories about environmental changes and historical events; songs of bitterness revealing misery and complaining oppression; agricultural songs reflecting nature and life experience; eulogies for beautiful scenery; ritual songs for receiving people and things; folk songs expressing traditional customs; sacrificial songs mourning; toast songs celebrating the full moon of marriage, the completion of new residence and the birthday of the elderly as well as love songs.

나파좡족민요는 그 민족의 생산로동, 일상생활, 명절활동 등에서 기원되였기에 생활정취가 풍부하다. 내용면에서 나포좡족 민요는 주로 신화, 전설, 인물전기, 환경변화, 역사사건 등을 서술한 노래로 구성되었다. 고난과 억압을 하소연하는 사랑의 노래; 자연과 생활 경험을 반영한 농사노래; 아름다운 경치를 동경하는 찬송가, 사람을 맞이하고 사물을 대하는 예의노래, 전통습관을 표현한 풍속노래, 장례를 위한 제사가, 결혼 1개월, 새집 낙성, 노인의 생신을 축하하는 축배 노래 및 내용이 풍부한 사랑 노래.

那坡壮民歌采用大量的夸张、比喻、拟人叠字、叠韵、双声等修辞手法，使山歌有优美的形式和丰富的内涵，或高亢嘹亮，或抒情委婉、犹如天籁之音，用歌词表达爱情、友情、祝愿、或其他生活的态度，体现出特有的山野风格与浓郁的壮族风情。

Napo folk songs of Zhuang adopt a large number of rhetorical devices such as exaggeration, metaphor, anthropomorphic overlapping characters, overlapping rhymes and double vocals, providing the folk songs with beautiful forms and rich connotations. Some songs are loud and clear, while others are lyrical and euphemistic, just like the sounds of nature. The lyrics express love, friendship, wishes or other attitudes towards life, reflecting the unique mountain and wild style and strong Zhuang customs.

그 언덕 장 민요를 대량의 과장, 비유, 의인 겹 글자 첩 운 쌍성 등 수법, 민요로 하여금 아름다운 형태와 풍부한 내포하거나 높고 낭랑하, 또는 서정 완곡하게, 마치 자연의 소리, 가사로 표현 사랑, 우정, 축원, 또는 기타 생활 태도를 보여주는 특유의 산야 풍 격과 쫭 족 풍정이 짙다.

Napo Zhuang folk songs adopt a large number of rhetorical devices such as exaggeration, metaphor, anthropomorphic overlapping characters, overlapping rhymes and double vocals, so that the folk songs have beautiful forms and rich connotations. Some songs are loud and clear, some are lyrical and euphemistic, just like the sounds of nature. The lyrics express love, friendship, wishes or other attitudes towards life, reflecting the unique mountain and wild style and strong Zhuang customs in Napo Zhuang folk songs.Napo Zhuang folk songs adopt a large number of rhetorical devices such as exaggeration, metaphor, anthropomorphic overlapping characters, overlapping rhymes and double vocals, so that the folk songs have beautiful forms and rich connotations. Some songs are loud and clear, some are lyrical and euphemistic, just like the sounds of nature. The lyrics express love, friendship, wishes or other attitudes towards life, reflecting the unique mountain and wild style and strong Zhuang customs in Napo Zhuang folk songs.Napo Zhuang folk songs adopt a large number of rhetorical devices such as exaggeration, metaphor, anthropomorphic overlapping characters, overlapping rhymes and double vocals, so that the folk songs have beautiful forms and rich connotations. Some songs are loud and clear, some are lyrical and euphemistic, just like the sounds of nature. The lyrics express love, friendship, wishes or other attitudes towards life, reflecting the unique mountain and wild style and strong Zhuang customs in Napo Zhuang folk songs.Napo Zhuang folk songs mainly include narrative songs of myths and legends, biographies of characters, as well as stories about environmental changes and historical events. There are songs of bitterness, agricultural songs, eulogies for beautiful scenery, ritual songs, and sacrificial songs. The most abundant are love songs, which contain more than 20 kinds of content, such as lyrics about first love, loyalty, separation, exhortation, regret, nostalgia, reunion, and bitterness. Napo Zhuang folk songs mainly include narrative songs of myths and legends, biographies of characters, as well as stories about environmental changes and historical events. There are songs of bitterness, agricultural songs, eulogies for beautiful scenery, ritual songs, and sacrificial songs. The most abundant are love songs, which contain more than 20 kinds of content, such as lyrics about first love, loyalty, separation, exhortation, regret, nostalgia, reunion, and bitterness. Napo Zhuang folk songs mainly include narrative songs of myths and legends, biographies of characters, as well as stories about environmental changes and historical events. There are songs of bitterness, agricultural songs, eulogies for beautiful scenery, ritual songs, and sacrificial songs. The most abundant are love songs, which contain more than 20 kinds of content, such as lyrics about first love, loyalty, separation, exhortation, regret, nostalgia, reunion, and bitterness.

在漫长的发展过程中，那坡壮族民歌形成了与民间习俗相依存、内容丰富多彩以及原生性等特征。除了具有交际、宣传、教育、娱乐等作用外，那坡壮族民歌同时具有历史价值、学术价值、艺术价值和实用价值，它是壮族远古歌谣文化的遗存。

In the long process of development, Napo folk song of Zhuang ethnic group has formed the characteristics of interdependence with folk customs, rich and colorful content and original ecology. Besides the functions of communication, propaganda, education and entertainment, it also has historical, academic, artistic and practical values, which are the relics of the ancient ballad culture of the Zhuang ethnic group.

기나긴 발전 과정에서 나포좡족 민요는 민간 풍속에 의존하면서 내용이 풍부하고 다채로우며 원시적인 특징을 형성하였다. 교제, 선전, 교육, 오락 등의 역할 외에도 나포좡족 민요는 역사적 가치, 학술적 가치, 예술적 가치, 실용적 가치를 동시에 지니고 있는 좡족 고대 가요문화의 유물이다.

8. 瑶族蝴蝶歌

Butterfly Song of Yao Ethnic Group
[入选时间：2008 Time: 2008
遗产名录：第一批国家级非物质文化遗产扩展项目名录
Heritage Category: Extended list of the first batch of National Intangible Cultural Heritage.
地域：贺州 Region: Hezhou]

瑶族蝴蝶歌流行于广西富川瑶族自治县、钟山县和湖南江华瑶族自治县及其毗邻等地的瑶族聚居区。因为在歌的衬字词中，常出现"蝴的蝶""蝶的蝶""黄蜂"之类衬词，故此得名"蝴蝶歌"。

Butterfly Song of Yao Ethnic Group is popular in Fuchuan Yao Autonomous County and Zhongshan County of Guangxi, Jianghua Yao Autonomous County of Hunan as well as its adjacent areas. Butterfly Song earns its name for the modal words of "butterfly" and "wasp" in the songs.

요족나비노래는 광시부천요족자치현, 종산현과 호남강화요족자치현 및 그 인접지역의 요족집거구에서 유행하였다. 노래의 부속단어 중에 "나비의 나비", "나비의 나비", "나비의 나비", "말벌" 같은 부속단어가 자주 나타나서 "나비 노래"라는 이름을 얻었다.

蝴蝶歌在瑶族二声部民歌中，用一种叫做"梧州土白话"的方言土语演唱，歌手们即兴创作、出口成章、一唱群和。歌词结构多为七言，联结四句成为一首。有时第三句后要扩充一个五字句，以强调歌手要表达的主要意思。歌词的内容多为抒情表意，或表达歌者对爱情、幸福的执著与向往，或表达歌者对时代、环境、人和事的褒奖与赞誉。蝴蝶歌节拍柔丽，抑扬顿挫，袅娜悠远，有极强的艺术感染力。

In the two-part duet of Yao folk songs, Butterfly Song is sang in Wuzhou Dialect, with the singers improvising and singing in groups. The structure of the lyrics is mostly four sentences of seven words in each and sometimes the third sentence followed by a five-word extension to emphasize the main idea the singer is trying to convey. The contents of the lyrics are mostly the expression of the singers' pursuit of love and happiness, and the singers' compliment to times, environment, people and things. Butterfly Song has a strong artistic appeal for its soft, graceful beat and cadence.

나비노래 요족 2 성부 민요에서' 오저우토백화(오오주토백화)'라는 방언의 토속어로 부르는데 가수들은 즉흥적으로 창작하고 그대로 읊어 문장을 만들고, 일창무리로 화음을 만들었다. 가사의 구조는 대부분 칠언이며 사구를 연결시켜 한 수를 이룬다. 때로는 세 번째 문장뒤에 다섯자구를 확충하여 가수가 표현하려는 주요 뜻을 강조하기도 한다. 가사의 내용은 대부분 감정을 표현하거나 사랑, 행복에 대한 가수의 집착과 갈망 또는 시대, 환경, 사람과 사물에 대한 가수의 칭찬과 찬양을 표현한다. 나비노래는 박자가 부드럽고 아름다우며 억양이 부드럽고 아담하며 아주 강한 예술적 감화력이 있다.

唱蝴蝶歌是瑶族人民生活中一种重要的文艺活动，是他们沟通心灵，交流经验的主要方式。瑶族的唱歌习俗遗存着浓厚的百越遗风，凡节日赶圩、婚嫁喜庆、礼仪交往等聚会活动，瑶族人无论男女老少都爱唱蝴蝶歌。蝴蝶歌在每年春季花开的时候唱得最盛，曲调清丽优美，婉转悠扬，悦耳动听，听之即有"余音绕梁，三日不绝"之感，堪称民歌中之奇葩。蝴蝶歌唱时发出的声音如昆虫翅膀舞动时发出的美妙之声，故被海内外人士称为"一支流淌于翅膀上的山歌"。

Singing Butterfly Song is an important activity in the lives of Yao people, which is a main way for them to communicate. There is a strong legacy of Baiyue in the singing customs of Yao Group. Yao people regardless of gender and age love singing Butterfly Song in their gatherings, such as fairs, weddings and parties. The most popular season for Butterfly Song is spring when flowers are in blossom. The graceful, melodious and pleasant tune leaves the effect of "sound lingering for three days", which makes it exotic among the folk songs. The sound produced in Butterfly Song singing is compared to the wonderful sound made by the insects while flapping their wings. Thus, Butterfly Song is named as "the folk song flowing on the wings".

나비노래를 부르는 것은 요족인민들의 생활가운데서 중요한 문예활동으로서 그들이 마음을 교류하고 경험을 교류하는 주요한 방식이다. 요족의 노래 풍속은 백월(百越)의 유풍이 짙게 남아 있는데, 무릇 명절날 장을 보러 가고, 혼사를 경축하고, 예절 교제 등 모임 활동에서 요족은 남녀노소를 막론하고 모두 나비노래를 부른다. 나비노래는 매년 봄 꽃이 필 때 가장 성행하는데 곡조가 청아하고 아름다우며, 구성지고 은은하여 듣기 좋으며, 들으면 바로 "여음이 맴돌면 사흘이 그치지 않는다"는 느낌을 주는데, 민요 중의 걸작이라 할 만하다. 나비가 노래할 때 나는 소리는 곤충이 날개짓할 때 나는 아름다운 소리와 같아서 국내외 사람들은 "날개에 흐르는 하나의 산노래"라고 부른다.

广西富川瑶族自治县是蝴蝶歌唱得最响亮、最动听的区域。当客人来瑶寨做客时,瑶哥瑶妹一首《流水欢歌迎客来》的蝴蝶歌会在村前唱响,客人进村时唱拦路酒歌,喝油茶时唱敬茶歌,客人走了唱送别歌。瑶族蝴蝶歌曲终歌未了,已经成了瑶族儿女日常生活中的一部分,也是瑶族人民口头文学中的一个组成部分。

Fuchuan Yao Autonomous County of Guangxi is the region where you can hear the most beautiful and pleasant Butterfly Song. Yao people will sing different forms of Butterfly Song to welcome guests:" Running Water welcoming guests" when guests in front of the village, "Road blocking wine song" when guests entering the village, "tea toast song" when guests drinking oil tea, and farewell song when guests leaving. Butterfly Song is a forever song and has been a part of Yao people's daily life and their oral literature.

광시 부천요족자치현은 나비가 가장 우렁차고 가장 듣기 좋은 구역이다. 손님이 요촌마을에 오면 요지와 요매는 "류수환가 손님맞이한다"는 나비노래를 마을앞에서 부르고 손님이 마을에 들어오면 길막이 술노래를 부르고 동백차를 마실 때는 권차 노래를 부르며 손님이 가면 송별노래를 부른다. 요족의 나비노래는 요족자녀들의 일상생활중의 일부분이 되였고 요족인민 구전문학의 한 구성부분으로 되였다.

9. 壮族三声部

Three-part Folk Song of Zhuang Ethnic Group
[入选时间: 2008 Time: 2008
遗产名录: 第一批国家级非物质文化遗产扩展项目名录
Heritage Category: Extended list of the first batch of National Intangible Cultural Heritage.
地域: 南宁　Region: Nanning]

壮族三声部民歌最早出现于唐宋，盛行于明清时期。属于广西北部壮族山歌，主要分布在广西马山县东部地区和上林县交界地带，有着浓厚的民族特色，旋律优美。

Three-part folk song of Zhuang first appeared in Tang and Song Dynasties and prevailed in Qing Dynasty. It belongs to the folk songs in the North of Guangxi, which mainly exists in the eastern part of Mashan County and the border region of Shanglin County and has strong national characteristics, beautiful melody.

쫭족의 3 성부 민요는 당송시기에 출현하여 명청시기에 흥행하였다. 주로 광서 마산현 동부지역과 상림현 접경지대에 분포되어 있으며, 민족특색이 짙고 선율이 아름답다.

壮族三声部民歌主旋律高亢明亮流畅，合声旋律婉转、柔和，唱法具有浓厚的原生态特点。歌曲由三个声部构成，三人以上演唱。第一声部为歌曲主旋律，由主唱者演唱；第二声部副旋律；第三声部为和声，由二人以上合唱。三个声部都能突出主旋律，第一、二声部独立音调，三声部起到陪衬和声作用。演唱时，时兴"哈"声，故又称"欢哈"("欢"，壮语为"山歌"）。

It has the feature of resonant and smooth main melody, pleasant and soft chorus and a singing method of original ecological characteristics. The song consists three parts and is sung by more than three people: the first part is the main melody, and sung by the lead singer; the second part is the secondary melody; the third part is the chorus and sung by more than two people. All the three parts can highlight the main melody, with the first and second part as the independent tune and the third part as the background tune. Due to its popular use of ha sound while singing, it is also called huanha (huan in Zhuang language means folk song).

쫭족 3성부 민요는 주선율이 높고 맑고 유창하며, 합성 선율이 완곡하고 부드러우며 창법이 원시적인 특징이 짙다. 노래는 3개 성부로 구성되며 3명 이상이 부른다. 제1성부는 노래의 주선율로서 주창자가 부르고, 제2성부는 부선율이고, 제3성부는 화성으로 2인 이상이 합창한다. 세 성부는 모두 주선율을 부각시킬 수 있으며, 제1성부와 제2성부는 음조를 독립시키고, 제3성부는 곁들여 화성 역할을 한다. 노래를 부를 때, "하"소리가 유행하여, "환하"라고도 부른다.

壮族三声部民歌的歌词一般有五言四句式和五三五言六句式，押韵严格。五言四句式歌词按普通壮歌押韵。五三五言六句式歌词押韵特殊，其歌词的第一句、第二句的末尾词与第三句的第三个词押韵，第四句、第五句的末尾词相互押韵，又与第六句的第三个词语押韵，故此类句式结构的山歌又称为"三顿欢"或"三跳欢"。中国民族音乐家范西姆在其著作《壮族三声部民歌》中详细介绍了该民歌。

The lyrics of Three-part folk song of Zhuang are generally divided into five-character-four-sentence pattern and five-three-five-character-six-sentence pattern, each of which has strict rhythm. The former has the same rhythm as the general Zhuang folk songs. The latter has a special rhythm, in which the ending words of the first and second sentence have the same rhythm with the third words in the third sentence, and the ending words of the fourth and sixth sentence not only have the same rhythm with each other but also with the third words in the sixth sentence. Thus, this kind of structured folk song is also named as "three pause huan" and "three jump huan". Chinese folk musician Fan Sim presented detailed introduction in his book *Zhuang Three-part Folk Song*.

좡족 3성부 민요의 가사는 일반적으로 5언 4구형과 5언 6구형이 있으며 압운이 엄격하다. 5언 4구형의 가사는 보통의 장가에 따라 압운한다. 535언 6구형의 가사 압운 특수, 그 가사의 첫 문장, 두 번째 절의 마지막 단어와 세 번째 절의 세 번째 단어, 네 번째, 다섯 절의 마지막 단어는 서로 압운, 그리고 여섯 절의 세 번째 단어와 압운, 따라서 이러한 구형 구조의 산 노래를 "삼둔환" 또는 "삼추환"이라고도 한다. 중국의 민족음악가 범심은 그의 저서 ≪좡족 3성부민가≫에서 이 민요를 상세하게 소개하였다.

壮族三声部民歌主要传唱于壮族社会的生活生产、交往娱乐、恋爱、婚丧和娱神等过程中,其中用于婚嫁、丧葬、娱神等仪式尤为庄重,被称作壮族民歌的"活化石",它的发现填补了东方少数民族没有多声部民歌的空白。其独特的演唱风格和艺术特点,被誉为"中华民歌艺术奇苑"。还曾受邀出访世界多个国家, 2013年壮族三声部民歌合唱团 被国家文化部选派参加"中国蒲公英(2013)维也纳金色大厅夏季音乐会",获得良好的世界声誉。

The three-part folk song of Zhuang is mainly sung in the process of Zhuang people's work and life, communication and entertainment, love and marriage, funeral and sacrifice, among which the song is solemnly performed in the ceremonies of marriage, funeral and sacrifice. Therefore, three-part folk song of Zhuang is considered as the living fossil of the folk songs of Zhuang ethnic group. Its discovery filled in the gap of the absence of multi-part folk songs in ethnic groups of eastern countries. Its unique singing style and artistic feature made it an exotic art of Chinese folk songs. It has also been invited to visit many countries in the world. In 2013, the Zhuang three-part folk Choir was selected by the Ministry of Culture to participate in the "Dandelion of China (2013) Summer Concert in Vienna's Musica Hall", and gained a good reputation in the world.

쫭족 3성부 민요는 주로 쫭족 사회의 생활 생산, 교제 오락, 연애, 혼례, 위신 등 과정에서 불려졌는데 그 중 혼인, 장례, 위신 등 의식이 특히 장중하여 쫭족 민요의 '활화석'으로 불린다. 이 민요의 발견은 동방 소수민족에 다성부 민요의 공백을 메웠다. 독특한 가창 풍격과 예술특성으로 "중화민요예술의 기원"으로 불린다. 2013년 중국 문화부에서" 중국 민들레 (2013) 비엔나 황금홀 여름음악회"에 참가하여, 좡족 3성부 민요 합창단은 세계 여러 나라를 방문하도록 초청받았으며, 세계적인 명성을 얻었다.

10. 广西八音

Guangxi Bayin music
[入选时间：2011 Time: 2011
遗产名录：第三批国家级非物质文化遗产扩展项目名录
Heritage Category: Extended list of the third batch of National Intangible Cultural Heritage.
地域：玉林　Region: Yulin]

"广西八音"又称"桂南八音",是中国民间器乐的一个乐种,主要流行于南宁、玉林、贵港、钦州、梧州、贺州等地的汉族、壮族、瑶族聚居地。它曲调优美、嘹亮,演奏风格热烈、欢快,富有广西地方民族特色,是广西颇有影响的民间器乐艺术,其中以玉林的八音最具代表性。

Guangxi Bayi music, also named as eight music of Southern Gui(short form of Guangxi), is one of the genres of Chinese folk instrumental music, mainly prevailing in Han-populated, Zhuang-populated and Yao-populated areas of the cities like Nanning, Yulin, Guigang, Qinzhou, Wuzhou and Hezhou. With the graceful and resonant tune, warm and pleasant performance style, and rich local ethnic features of Guangxi, Guangxi Bayin is an influential folk instrumental art in Guangxi, among which Yulin Bayin hosts the most representative Bayin music.

'광시팔음'은 '계남팔음'이라고도 하는데, 중국 민간 기악의 악종으로 주로 난닝·위린·귀항·친저우·오주·하주 등지의 한족·좡족·요족 집단 거주지에서 유행한다. 곡조가 아름답고 우렁차며, 연주풍격이 열렬하고 경쾌하여 광서지방의 민족특색이 짙다. 광시에서 영향력이 큰 민간기악 예술로서 옥림(玉林)의 팔음(八音)이 가장 대표적이다.

据考证,广西八音源自秦汉时期的宫廷和军中的吹鼓乐,距今已有近千年的历史。相传明崇祯年间,一个在宫廷抄誊乐谱的九品笔吏告老还乡,回到玉林米粉新村后,将他带回来的乐谱和宫廷的演奏法与当时民间音乐相结合,初步整理、形成了独具特色的"玉林八音"。清乾隆年间,《九宫大成南北词谱》流传到玉林、博白、陆川、兴业、福绵等地，客家人把赣、闽、粤等地的吹打乐带了进来，使桂东南玉林八音发展迅速。此后，乐师们又不断从当时乡村流行的玉林民歌、采茶调中吸收精华，从而确定下了今天玉林八音的基调。到了晚清时期，八音已在玉林极为盛行。

According to textual research, Guangxi Bayin originated from the wind and drum music performed in court and military in Qin and Han Dynasties, and had a history of nearly thousand years. Legend has it that in Chongzhen Emperor Period of Ming Dynasty, there was a retired *Jiupin* pen officer (ninth grade of ranks in Chinese Feudal regimes) whose job was to copy musical scores in the imperial court returned his home in Mifen New Village in Yulin. He combined the imperial musical scores and performing styles with that of the folk music at that time. After preliminary edit, the unique Yulin Bayin music was formed. During the period of Qianlong Emperor of Qing Dynasty, the Comprehensive Notation for Southern and Northern Ci Poetry was spread to Yulin, Bobai, Luchuan, Xingye, Fumian and other regions. The Hakka brought the wind and percussion music from Jiangxi, Fujian, Guangdong and other places, which led to the rapid development of Yulin Bayin in the Southeast of Gui. After that, the musicians continued to absorb the essence from the popular Yulin folk songs and tea tunes in the countryside at that time, which leads to the determination of the basic tone of

Today's Yulin Bayin. By the late Qing Dynasty, Bayin music had been very popular in Yulin.

고증에 따르면, 광서의 팔음은 진한시기 궁정과 군중의 취고악에서 기원하였는데 지금으로부터 이미 근 천년의 역사를 갖고 있다. 명나라 숭전(崇典) 연간에 궁중에서 악보를 베끼던 9품 필기 관리가 노예를 고하고 고향으로 돌아왔는데, 위린(玉林) 미편(米粉) 신촌에 돌아온 후 그가 가지고 온 악보와 궁중의 연주법을 당시의 민간 음악과 결합하여 초보적으로 정리하면서 독특한 "위린(玉林) 8음"을 형성했다고 한다. 청나라 건륭 연간에 「구궁대성남북사보」가 옥림(玉林), 박백(博白), 육천(六川), 흥업(興業), 복면(福面) 등지에 전해졌고, 객가인들이 강서(甘西), 민서(民西), 광동(廣東) 등지의 취타악을 들여와 광서(廣西) 동남부 옥림(玉林) 팔음은 빠른 발전을 가져왔다. 그 후 악사들은 또 당시 농촌에서 유행되던 옥림민요(玉林民歌)와 채차조 (彩茶調)에서 부단히 정수를 받아들여 오늘날의 옥림팔음(玉林八音)의 기조를 확정하였다. 청조말기에 이르러 팔음은 이미 옥림에서 매우 성행하였다.

广西八音因使用鼓、锣、钹、笛、箫、弦、琴、梆子等八种乐器演奏而得名"八音"，曲调以五声调式为主，曲牌主要有"套牌"、"吹场"和"牌子"。它每个乐班（队）由6-8人组成，在演奏曲目、程序和乐器分工上很有讲究。在演奏前要根据服务的对象和演奏场合，选择相应的红事、白事或中性曲目，按"龙头"、"虎腰"、"凤尾"这三个曲目程序进行演奏。

Guangxi Bayin music earned its name for the eight instruments played in its performance, including, drum, gong, cymbal, flute, *xiao*, strings, *qin* and clapper. It is majorly five-toned tune and has the name of the tunes such as set, wind field, brand. Each of its musical team consists six to eight members, who are very particular about the repertoire, procedures and division of the musical instruments. Before performing, the music tracks need to be selected among wedding music, funeral music and neutral music according to the audience type and performing occasions, and performed according three steps, namely "dragon head", "tiger waist" and "phoenix tail".

광시팔음은 북·징·동발·피리·소·현·거문고·방자 등 8가지 악기로 연주하기 때문에 '팔음'이라는 이름을 얻었으며, 곡조는 오성조 형식을 위주로 하고, 곡패에는 주로 '투패', '취장', '패'가 있다. 각 악반(팀)은 6~8명으로 구성되며, 연주곡과 프로그램, 악기 분류가 정교하다. 연주 전, 봉사하는 대상과 연주 장소에 따라 상응하는 성사, 성사 혹은 중성 곡목을 선택하여 '용두', '호허리', '봉미' 등 3가지 곡목 순서를 따라 연주한다.

广西八音在演奏种类上因地域的不同而分为玉林软场八音、硬场八音和南宁壮族文场八音、武场八音等。在演奏形式上以合奏的形式来表现，主要有坐奏和行奏。在音乐功能上主要用于民间新居落成、婚娶、丧葬、祝寿、开业、节庆、迎宾等民间、民俗活动，也为舞龙、舞狮、民间戏曲、舞蹈伴奏。广西八音音乐表现力十分丰富，艺术生命力较强，深受人民群众所喜爱。

In performing types, Guangxi Bayin music can be classified into Soft Bayin and hard Bayin of Yulin, Civil Bayin and Military Bayin of Nanning Zhuang ethnic group and other types. As to the performing forms, Guangxi Bayin music is mainly played by ensemble and can be divided into two major types: one is the "sitting type" and the other the "walking type". Guangxi Bayin music can be performed in the following folk ceremonies such as new house completion, wedding, funeral, old people birthday, business opening, festivals and guests welcoming. It can also be used to accompany dragon and lion dances, folk operas and dances. With its rich musical expressiveness and strong artistic vitality, Guangxi Bayin music is deeply loved by the ordinary people.

광시팔음은 연주 종류에 있어서 지역에 따라 위린연창팔음, 경창팔음과 난닝좡족문창팔음, 무창팔음 등으로 나뉜다. 연주형식에서는 합주의 형식으로 표현되는데 주로 좌주와 행주가 있다. 음악 기능상 주로 민간의 새집 낙성, 결혼, 장례, 축수, 개업, 축제, 환영 등 민간, 민속 활동에 사용되고 용춤, 사자춤, 민간 희곡, 무용 반주하기도 한다. 광서의 팔음음악은 표현력이 아주 풍부하고 예술생명력이 강해 대중의 사랑을 많이 받는다.

11. 京族独弦琴艺术

Single-stringed Fiddle Art of Jing Ethnic Group

[入选时间：2011　Time: 2011

遗产名录：第三批国家级非物质文化遗产名录

Heritage Category: Extended list of the third batch of National Intangible Cultural Heritage.

地域：防城港　Region: Fangchenggang]

京族独弦琴，属弹拨类弦鸣乐器，因独有一根弦而被世人习称为独弦琴。在京族民间称匏琴，或称独弦匏琴，京族语即直呼旦匏，是我国古代流传下来的一种古老乐器。独弦琴艺术是我国唯一的海洋性民族——京族所拥有的传统音乐艺术，主要分布于广西东兴市京族聚居区。京族独弦琴艺术主要包括独弦琴制作技艺和独弦琴演奏艺术。

Single-stringed Fiddle of Jing Ethnic Group, a plucked musical instrument earned its name for its unique one string. Known as Paoqin or single-stringed pao in Jing folk, and Danpao in Jing Language, it is an old instrument handed down since ancient China. Single-stringed Fiddle Art is a traditional musical art owned by the Jing ethnic group, which is the only ocean minority in China, prevailing in the Jing-populated areas of Dongxing Guangxi. Single-stringed Fiddle Art of Jing mainly includes the making art and performing art of single-stringed fiddle.

징족독현악기는 타발류 현울기에 속하며 단 하나의 현만 가지고 있어 세인들은 독현악기라고 부른다. 징족민간에서는 파금 또는 독현파금이라고 하는데 징족어로 직접 단파라고 부르는데 우리나라에서 고대로부터 전해내려 온 오래된 악기이다. 독현악예술은 우리나라의 유일한 해양성 민족인 징족의 전통음악예술로서 주로 광서 동흥시 징족집거구에 분포되어 있다. 징족독현악예술에는 주로 독현악제작기교와 독현악연주예술이 포함된다.

京族独弦琴因制作材质不同而分为竹制和木制两种。竹制独弦琴,琴身采用一截粗大的毛竹筒制作,琴面钻一个穿弦小孔,内侧立一竹制琴马,琴底置一木制弦轴,插入竹制摇杆,摇杆下端横置去底的小葫芦做的共鸣筒。木制独弦琴,琴身由面板、底板和框板胶合而成,外观呈不规则的长方形匣状,琴面宽的一端为琴首,琴面窄的一端为琴尾。

Single-stringed Fiddle of Jing can be divided into bamboo-made and wood made. The bamboo made single-stringed fiddle has the following features: the body of the fiddle is made of a thick bamboo tube; on the surface of the fiddle, there is a drilled hole for inserting the string and a bamboo made fiddle bridge erected inside of it; a wooden shaft is set on the bottom of the fiddle, and a bamboo made rocker is inserted, below which a bottomless small calabash is flatly set for resonator. As for the wood made single-stringed fiddle, the body of the instrument is a glued structure of three panels: surface, bottom and frame, whose appearance is like an irregular rectangular box; the surface of the instrument has the broad end as the head of the fiddle and the narrow end the tail.

징족독현금은 제작 재질에 따라 죽제와 목제 두 종류로 나뉜다. 대나무독현악기는 몸체는 굵은 죽통으로 만들고 면에 현을 뚫는 구멍을 뚫은 후 안쪽에는 대나무말을 세운다. 밑바닥에는 나무현축을 설치하여 대나무조이스틱에 꽂고 조이스틱의 하단에는 밑바닥에 작은 박이 가로로

된 공명통이 놓여있다. 목제 독현악기는 몸체가 판넬, 바닥판, 골반의 합으로 되어 있고, 모양이 불규칙한 장방형 상자 모양이며, 얼굴의 넓은 한쪽 끝이 끝이 머리이고, 얼굴의 좁은 한쪽 끝이 꼬리이다.

在历史发展过程中，京族虽然受到了汉族、壮族民族文化的影响，但其独弦琴演奏艺术却一直保持着较为浓郁的本民族特色。独弦琴演奏具有坐式和站式两种姿势。演奏时，多将琴横置于桌子、架子或双腿上，或将琴尾置于腿上，琴头放置于地面或架子上，右手持挑棒或竹签弹奏，左手握摇杆，通过推、拉改变弦的张力和长度，以获得不同的音高。京族独弦琴的演奏技巧十分丰富，常用的弹奏方法主要有正弹法、反弹法、刮奏、击奏、点奏等。

In the course of historical development, though influenced by the culture Han and Zhuang groups, Single-stringed Fiddle Art of Jing has maintained its strong national characteristics. It has two performing postures: sitting and standing. While playing, the performers put the fiddle horizontally on the table, shelf or their legs, or put the tail of the fiddle on the legs and the head of the fiddle on the floor or shelf, with right hand holding the pick stick or bamboo stick to play and left hand holding the rocker to change the tension and length of the string by pulling and pushing so as to get different pitches. Single-stringed Fiddle Art of Jing has different performing skills, and the commonly used ones are the forward playing, the backward playing, scratch playing, percussion playing and the point playing.

역사 발전 과정에서 징족은 비록 한족과 쫭족의 민족 문화의 영향을 받았지만 독현악기 연주 예술은 줄곧 비교적 강한 본 민족의 특색을 유지하고 있다. 독현악기 연주는 좌식과 서식의 두 가지 자세가 있다. 연주할 때 주로 하모니를 테이블, 선반 또는 다리 위에 가로놓거나 하모니를 다리 위에 올리고 하모니를 지면이나 선반 위에 놓으며 오른손으로 막대기나 꼬챙이로 연주하고 왼손으로 조이스틱을 잡고 밀거나 당겨서 현의 장력과 길이를 변화시켜 다른 음높이를 얻는다. 징족 독현악기의 연주 기교는 매우 풍부하며, 자주 사용하는 연주 방법에는 주로 정탄법, 반탄법, 스크래치, 타주, 점주 등이 있다.

独弦琴是京族传统文化的精华, 是京族人民知识、智慧和技能的载体, 同时也是团结京族人民, 增强京族社会认同感与凝聚力的重要渠道。

Single-stringed Fiddle Art of Jing is the essence of the traditional culture of the Jing people, as well as the carrier of Jing people's knowledge, wisdom and skills. It is also an important channel to unite Jing people and enhance their sense of social identity and cohesion.

독현악기는 징족 전통문화의 정화이고 징족 인민의 지식, 지혜와 기능을 담으며 또한 징족 인민을 단결시키고 징족 사회의 동질감과 응집력을 증강시키는 중요한 경로이다.

12. 田林瑶族铜鼓舞

Tianlin Bronze Drum Dance of Yao Ethnic Group
[入选时间：2008　Time: 2008
遗产名录：第一批国家级非物质文化遗产扩展项目名录
Heritage Category: Extended list of the first batch of National Intangible Cultural Heritage.
地域： 百色　　Region: Baise]

田林瑶族铜鼓舞属于自称"诺莫",他称"木柄瑶"、"长发瑶"支系的瑶族民族民间舞蹈。据《田林县志》记载,木柄瑶自称铜鼓是老祖宗从贵州迁来时带来的,是深受广大瑶族人民喜爱的地方艺术。它流传于田林县潞城瑶族乡三瑶村的瑶怒屯,至今已有二百多年的历史。

Tianlin Bronze Drum Dance of Yao Ethnic Group is the folk dance of the branch of Long hair Yao, who called themselves "Nuomo" and was called "wooden handle Yao". According to records of Tianlin Couny Annals, "wooden handle Yao" claimed that the bronze drum was brought to Tianlin by their ancestors from Guizhou province. It is a local art deeply loved by Yao people, prevailing in Yaonu tun of Sanyao village in Lucheng Yao township of Tianlin County and has a history of more than 200 years.

톈린요족(田林瑶族) 동북춤은 자칭 '노모(nomo)'라고 하고, 그는 '목빙요(木平요우)', '창발요(長발요)' 계통이라고 부르는 요족 민속 무용이다. ≪전림현지≫의 기재에 따르면 목병요는 동고는 조상들이 귀주에서 이주해올 때 가져온 것이며 광범한 요족인민들의 사랑을 받는 지방예술이라고 주장하였다. 전림현 로성요족향 삼요촌의 요노툰(瑶노툰)에서 전해지고 있는데 지금까지 이미 200여 년의 역사를 갖고 있다.

瑶族铜鼓舞的表演需要一大一小两面铜鼓,大鼓为公鼓,小鼓为母鼓,两面铜鼓大小差异不大,鼓面直径大约在45厘米左右;挂在鼓架上时,公鼓在左，母鼓在右。除了铜鼓，还有一只长约80厘米、鼓面直径约30厘米的长鼓。此外还有铜鼓鼓槌、木鼓鼓槌若干根以及长号、唢呐、笛子、小鼓、锣、钹等乐器。舞蹈的基本动作有跨步反身击鼓、转身跨步击鼓、转身跨步跳跃击横杠、转身脑后击棍、转身背击棍、转身跨腿击棍等。转身是关键动作，跨步是基本步伐，手持鼓棍上扬击鼓是基本形态，相互结合就构成一种力量外溢的动律感。

The performance of Yao Bronze drum dance requires two drums, the bigger one as the male drum and the smaller one the female drum. The two drums has no distinct difference in size with a diameter of about 45 cm, while being hung on the drum rack, male drum is put on the left and the female on the right. In addition to the bronze drum, there is a long drum with a length of 80cm and a diameter of 30cm. Besides drums, there are also several drum sticks for both bronze and wooded drums, as well as other instruments like trombone, suona, flute, small drum, gong, cymbals. The basic movements of the dance include stepping and beating the drum, turning and beating the drum, turning, stepping, jumping and beating the drum, turning and beating the bar behind the head, turning and beating the bar at the back, turning and beating the bar across the legs. Among these movements, turning is considered as the key movement, stepping the basic step, and beating the drum with a rising stick the basic form, and the combination forms a dynamic sense of force overflowing.

요족동북춤은 1~2면의 동고가 필요한데 큰고는 공고, 작은고는 어머니고이다. 두면 동고의 크기는 큰 차이가 없고 북면의 직경은 약 45cm 가량이다. 고대에 걸 때 수고는 왼쪽에, 암고는 오른쪽에 둔다. 동고 외에 길이 80cm, 북 직경 30cm 정도의 장고도 있다. 이외에도 동고 북채, 목고 북채 몇 개 그리고 트롬본, 수르나이이, 피리, 소고, 징, 심벌즈 등의 악기가 있다. 춤의 기본동작은 보폭 뒤돌아서 북 치기, 돌아서서 보폭 뛰어서 북 치기, 돌아서 보폭 뛰어서 바 치기, 돌아서 뒤통수 치기, 돌아서 등 뒤통수 치기, 돌아서 다리 걸치고 치기 등이다. 몸을 돌리는 것이 관건적인 동작이고 보폭하는 것은 기본적인 보폭이며 손에 고봉을 들고 북을 오르내린 것은 기본 형태인데 서로 결합되면 힘이 밖으로 흘러 넘치는 동률감을 형성한다.

瑶族人民认为铜鼓是具有生命的灵物，跳铜鼓舞的时候，一定要举行祭鼓仪式。根据祖辈流传下来的习俗，仪式主要包括起鼓、祭鼓、打鼓、埋鼓等内容。起鼓又称请鼓，每年农历年三十晚上或者正月初二，田林瑶族村寨男女老少都要穿上节日盛装，由族中长老主持，举行一年一度的"起宝"仪式，把一公一母的两个铜鼓挖出来，用煮粽子的水洗干净，然后敲鼓三下表示请鼓结束。祭鼓时将铜鼓、木鼓、鼓架和鼓槌放置岑王大将军庙中，摆上香案，供上供品。祭完铜鼓后，主持人便指挥寨中青年把三面鼓挂起来。由主祭人先打一轮，之后别人才能轮流着打。鸣鼓开始时，动作缓慢轻柔，之后逐渐加快，鼓点高亢激昂，最后如疾风骤雨。两位敲牛皮鼓的是领舞者，他们边打边舞，时而正面打，时而转身打，铜锤不停地从自己的脑后、腰后、胯下挥过，在鼓面上轮流敲击，节奏鲜明，动作协调，天衣无缝。这时，场上的男女老少也纷纷加入舞蹈行列，人数不限，场面壮观，热烈奔放。先跳《圆圈舞》，依次跳《迎春舞》《扁担舞》，风格独特，舞姿优美，令人心悦神爽。每年跳完铜鼓，又将铜鼓埋入地下，留待来年跳铜鼓舞的时候再起鼓。

Yao people believe that the bronze drum is an object with living spirit, thus demanding a strict sacrificial ceremony while dancing. According to the customs handed down from the ancestors, the ceremony mainly includes "opening the drum", "sacrificing the drum", "beating the drum" and "burying the drum". Every year on the Chinese New Year's eve or on the second day of the first lunar month, men, women and children of Yao ethnic group are required to put on their festival costumes to attend the yearly "treasure opening ceremony presided by the elder of the group, on which the male and female drum will be dug out and washed with water which is used to boil Zongzi. Then beat the drum for three times to signal the end of the opening ceremony. In the process of "sacrificing the drum", bronze drums, wooden drum, drum stands and drumsticks are placed in the temple of General Cen Wang, and the sacrificial table is set. After the sacrifice of the bronze drum, the host will command the young men in the village to hang the drums on the rack and only after the chief priest played one round that others could started beating in turns. The beating starts slowly and gently, then gradually picks up speed, and reaches at its pitch like storms. The two players beating the cowhide drum are the leading players, who dance as playing in different postures varying from front beating to turning around beating, with the drum sticks swinging from the back of their head and waist as well as crossing their legs. They seamlessly take turns to beat the drums and produce a clear rhythm. At this moment, everyone present, who are not fixed in number will join the dance, creating a spectacular and enthusiastic scene. The drum dance starts from "circle dance", then "welcoming spring dance" and "shoulder pole dance", and the unique and graceful dances make people delighted and excited. Each year, after the drum dance, the drum will be buried in a rarely known location, waiting for next year's ritual.

요족 사람들은 동고는 생명을 가진 영물이기 때문에 동으로 춤을 출 때 반드시 북에 제를 지내는 의식을 거행해야 한다고 여긴다. 조상 대대로 전해 내려오는 풍습에 따르면 의식에는 주로 북 치기, 제북, 북 치기, 장고 등이 있다. 부터 북 하세요 북 이라고도 하는데 매년 음력 섣달 그믐날 저녁이나 정월 초 이튿날, 톈린요 족 마을 남녀노소 모두 명절 성장(Sheng 裝)을 입고 족에서 장로 주재로 열린 연례부터 바 오'식을 한 공정 한 어머니에게서 태어난 두 가 뽑아와 서 종자를 삶은 물로 깨끗하게, 그리고 북을 세 번 북 마무리를 밝 힌 바 있다. 제고할 때는 동고, 목고, 고대와 북채를 잠왕장군묘에 놓고 향안을 차려 놓고 공물을 올린다. 동고에 제를 올린 후 사회자가 마을 청년들을 지휘하여 삼면고를 걸었다.(주) 제자가 먼저 한 차례 치고 난 후에 다른 사람들이 교대로 치는 것이다.북소리는 처음에는 동작이 느리고 부드러우다가 후에는 점차

빨라지며 북소리는 높고 격앙되며 나중에는 질풍노도처럼 격렬하다. 소가죽북을 치는 두 사람은 리드댄서이다. 그들은 때로는 정면으로, 때로는 돌아서서 치며, 구리 망치를 자신의 머리 뒤와 허리 뒤, 가랑이 밑으로 끊임없이 휘두르며 북 위에서 번갈아 친다. 리듬이 선명하고 동작이 조화로우며 완벽하다. 이때 공연장의 남녀노소도 분분히 무용행렬에 참가하였는데 인원수를 제한하지 않았으며 장면이 장관이였으며 열렬하고 분방하였다. 먼저 ≪강강술래≫를 추고 차례로 ≪영춘무≫, ≪멜대춤≫을 추는데 풍격이 독특하고 춤자태가 아름다워 사람을 즐겁게 한다. 해마다 동고를 다 추고 나면 또 땅속에 파묻어버렸다가 다음 해에 동고무를 출 때 다시 북을 친다.

木柄瑶铜鼓舞有深刻的思想性和鲜明的艺术特征，其丰富的内容和传承历史，在中华民族文艺百花园中实属罕见，具有广泛的语言、文学、美学、音乐、艺术等研究价值。

The bronze dance of "wooden handle Yao" has profound thought and distinct artistic characteristics. Its rich content and inherited history is rare in Chinese national literature and art, thus having research values in the fields of language, literature, esthetics, music and art.

목병요동북춤은 깊은 사상성과 선명한 예술특징을 지니고 있으며, 그 풍부한 내용과 전승역사는 중화민족 문예의 백화원에서는 보기 드문 것으로 언어, 문학, 미학, 음악, 예술 등 광범위한 연구가치를 지니고 있다.

13. 瑶族长鼓舞

Long Drum Dance of Yao Ethnic Group
[入选时间：2008　Time: 2008
遗产名录：第二批国家级非物质文化遗产名录
Heritage Category: List of the second batch of National Intangible Cultural Heritage.
地域：贺州　Region: Hezhou]

瑶族长鼓舞是瑶族最具代表性的舞蹈。瑶语称为"播公"，历史悠久，距今已有800多年的历史。瑶族长鼓舞流行于广东、广西、湖南等省瑶族聚居地区，多在瑶族传统节日、庆祝丰收、乔迁或是婚礼喜庆的日子表演，在瑶族传统的祭盘王仪典中和在一些占卜活动中也常跳此舞。

Long drum dance is a most representative folk dance of Yao ethnic group, and it is called Bogong in Yao language, with a history of 800 years. It is enjoyed by a wide population throughout Yao-populated areas in Guangdong, Guangxi and Hunan provinces. Long drum dance of Yao is often performed in the following occasions: traditional Yao festivals, celebrations like harvest, housewarming and wedding, traditional sacrificial rituals of Panwang, and divination activities such as driving away devils and healing.

요족 장구춤은 요족의 가장 대표적인 무용이다. 야오어로 "파공"이라고 부르는데, 지금으로부터 800여 년의 역사를 가지고 있는 유구한 역사를 가지고 있다. 요족 장구춤은 광둥(廣東) 성, 광시(廣西) 성, 후난(湖南) 성 등 요족 집거 지역에서 유행하며, 요족 전통 명절, 풍작 경축, 집들이 또는 결혼식 때 공연되고, 요족 전통 제사(帝事)인 반왕(盘王)의 의식, 일부 점술 행사 등에서도 자주 춤을 춘다.

有关长鼓舞来历的传说，相传远古时瑶族始祖盘王有一次进山打猎，不幸被野羊撞死在空桐树下，盘王六个儿子闻讯赶来，含着悲奋之力追捕野羊，为父报仇。他们砍倒空桐树挖成长鼓，剥野羊皮蒙其鼓面，击鼓起舞而祭奠盘王。此后瑶族后裔每当"还盘王愿"时皆沿用这一仪式祀祖先。

There is a legend about the origin of the long drum dance. It is said that the ancient Yao ancestor Pan Wang once went into the mountains for hunting, and he was unfortunately killed by wild sheep under the tung tree. Pan Wang's six sons heard the news, and came with furious force to take revenge for the father by catching the wild sheep. They cut down the tung trees to dig long drums, peeled wild sheep skins to cover the drums, and beat drums and danced in honor of Pan King. Since then, the descendants of the Yao people always perform long drum dance to worship their ancestors whenever they "return the wish of Pan Wang".

장구흥의 유래에 관한 전설을 보면 태고적에 요족의 시조인 반왕이 사냥을 나갔다가 불행히 들양에 치여 오동나무밑에서 죽었다고 한다. 이 소식을 들은 반왕의 여섯 아들은 비분하여 들양을 쫓아 아버지의 원수를 대주었다.그들은 텅 빈 동나무를 베어 장북을 파고 들양의 가죽을 벗겨 북탈을 씌우고 북을 치며 춤을 추며 반왕에게 제사를 지냈다. 이후 요족(瑤族)의 후예들은 "환반왕원(환반왕원)"을 할 때마다 이 의식으로 조상들을 모셨다.

瑶族长鼓通常用沙桐木作材料，牛、羊皮蒙鼓面。长约1.2米左右，中间小两头大，其中一头又略大三分之一。木心挖空，两头蒙上精制过的黄羊皮，然后用6至8条染色麻绳拉紧两头黄羊皮，再涂上红、黄、白等色彩，绘上龙凤图案，美化鼓身。跳舞时，舞者用一条彩带绑着两头"鼓颈"，挂在肩上，横于腰间，右手使掌、左手持竹片分别击鼓，随着音乐节拍，即发出"唪啪唪梆"的铿锵之声。如果4人以上击鼓，随着音乐节拍，即发出"噼啪蓬平"的浑厚激昂之声。如果再配上牛角、芒锣、唢呐伴奏，声音效果则像古代列队排阵厮杀，鼓角喧天，振奋人心。

Long drum of Yao is usually made of Shatong wood and hides of cow and sheep. The drum is about 1.2 meters long and the middle part is smaller than that of the ends, with one end about one-third bigger than the other. To make the drum, the wood needs to be hollowed first, and two ends covered by fine made yellow sheep hide which is tightened by 6 to 8 pieces of dyed hemp strings, then painted in color of red, yellow and white, and at last dragon and phoenix pattern is added to beautify the drum. When dancing, the performers carry the drum which is tied by a ribbon between the two "drum necks" over their shoulders and waists, and beat the drum with both right hand palm and the bamboo chip held in the left hand, producing the loud and rhythmic sound of "peng pa peng bang". When there are more than four players, the loud and passionate sound of "pi pa peng ping" can be achieved. If accompanied by ox horn, mang gong and suona, a sound effect of ancient soldiers fighting in rows, clamorous horn sound echoed in the valley could be achieved, making people excited.

요족(瑤族)의 장고는 보통 사동목을 재료로 하고, 소·양가죽 등을 써서 북을 덮었다. 길이는 1.2m가량이고 가운데 작은 두 마리가 크고 그중의 한 마리는 3분의 1이 좀 더 크다. 목심을 파내고 양 끝을 정제해 만든 황색 양가죽으로 덮는다. 그리고 6~8가닥의 염색을 한 삼끈으로 황색 양피를 잡아당긴 다음 다시 적색, 황색, 백색 등 색채를 칠하고 용과 봉황 도안을 그려 북통을 아름답게 단장한다. 춤을 출 때, 무용수는 오색 띠로 양쪽의 '북목'을 묶고, 어깨에 걸고, 허리에 가로놓으며, 오른손으로는 손뼉을, 왼손으로는 대나무 조각을 들고 각각 북을 친다. 음악 박자에 따라 '큰소리로 탕, 큰소리로 탕'이라는 낭랑한 소리가 난다. 4명 이상이 북을 치면 음악의 박자에 따라 "와당탕펑핑"이라는 우렁차고 격앙된 소리가 난다. 여기에 뉴자오, 멍징, 수르나이 반주를 곁들이면 마치 고대처럼 대열을 지어 싸움을 벌이는 듯한 음향효과를 낼 수 있다.

瑶族长鼓舞分"单人舞""双人舞""群舞"等类型, 以独特的击鼓节奏, 刚劲敏捷的舞蹈动作, 反映瑶家人的生产斗争和生活习俗, 在表演形式和程式上, 都充分表现瑶胞的性格特征和气质, 是千百年来瑶族同胞生产生活的积淀和智慧的结晶。瑶族长鼓舞现在已经成为瑶族人民群众性的文娱活动, 在节日、婚事、宗教、丧葬等各种场合喜闻乐见, 热闹非常。

Long drum dance of Yao can be divided into types of "solo dance", "couple dance" and "group dance", etc.. It presents the customs of Yao people's work and life by way of its unique beating tempo and vigorous and agile movements. Its performing forms and patterns provides a full display of Yao people's characteristics and temperaments, making it a product of Yao people's wisdom and accumulated experiences in working life over hundreds of years. Nowadays, the long drum dance of Yao has become a public recreational activity, which is popularly and lively performed in the occasions of festivals, weddings, funerals, and religious rituals.

요족장구춤은 "독인무", "2인무", "군무" 등 류형으로 나뉘며 독특한 북치기 리듬과 강하고 민첩한 춤동작을 취한다. 요족 사람들의 생산투쟁과 생활풍속을 반영하고 공연 형식과 격식에서 요족 동포들의 성격특징과 기질을 충분히 표현하였는데 이는 천백 년 동안 요족 동포들이 생산과 생활에서 축적해 온 지혜의 결정체이다. 요족장구춤은 현재 이미 요족 인민들의 대중적인 문화오락활동으로 명절, 혼사, 종교, 장례 등 장소에서 즐겨 보는 것이 되어 매우 떠들썩하다.

14. 藤县狮舞

Lion Dance of Teng County

[入选时间: 2011 Time: 2011
遗产名录: 第三批国家级非物质文化遗产扩展项目名录
Heritage Category: Extended list of the third batch of National Intangible Cultural Heritage.
地域: 梧州　Region: Wuzhou]

藤县狮舞是一种古老的传统舞蹈，是梧州市藤县的汉族传统民俗文化活动，属于广东佛山流派的狮形和七星鼓点。藤县狮舞以高桩舞狮的高难度动作、独桩挟腰转体450°等绝技，名扬世界，享有"世界狮王"之美誉。

As an old traditional dance, the lion dance of Teng County is a folk activity of Han group tradition in Teng County Wuzhou City, which belongs to the "lion and seven star drum" of Foshan school in Guangdong. The lion dance of Teng County is famous around the world and gains a reputation of "Lion King of the World" for its difficult stunts such as high-stake lion dance and 450 degree waist rotation on a single stake.

등현의 사자춤은 오랜 전통무용으로서 오주시 등현의 한족전통민속문화활동이며 광동성 불산류파의 사자모양과 칠성북소리에 속한다. 후지현의 사자춤은 높은 말뚝으로 사자를 춤추는 고난도 동작과 하나의 말뚝으로 허리를 끼고 450° 몸을 돌리는 등 묘기로 세계에 널리 알려졌으며 '세계의 사자왕'이라는 명성을 가지고 있다.

从二十世纪八十年代中期至九十年代中期藤县蒙江村狮队技艺最高，影响力最大。蒙江狮队以狮形神态逼真、演技精湛，"大头佛"幽默诙谐、搞笑让人折服，以服装统一，阵势威武庞大而威振四方，狮子"吃"炮仗更是该队最过硬的本领。该狮队出游时旌旗招展，锣鼓喧天，群狮起舞，常引起万人空巷围观。

From the mid 1980s to the mid 1990s, the lion team of Mengjiang Village in Teng County had the highest skills and was the most influential one. It convinces people for its life-like lion, superb acting skills and funny "big head Buddha", and shocks people for its uniform costumes and mightily huge formation. The most excellent skill of the team is "lion eating firecrackers". When the lion team of Mengjiang village marches, a spectacular scene with flags and banners flying, drums and gongs thunderously beating, and group of lions dancing together will attract a crowds of onlookers.

20세기 80년대 중반부터 90년대 중반까지 등현 몽강촌의 사자팀이 기량이 가장 높고 영향력이 가장 컸다. 몽강사자팀은 사자 모양으로 생동감 있고 연기가 뛰어나다. "대두불 (大头佛)"은 해학적이고 익살스러워서 사람들을 납득시킬 수 있다. 복장은 통일되었고 진형은 위풍당당하여 사방을 휘어잡았다. 사자대가 여행을 떠날 때면 기발이 펄럭이고 꽹과리와 북소리가 하늘을 진동하며 사자무리들이 춤을 추는데 수많은 사람들이 모여들어 구경하였다.

藤县舞狮属南派舞狮，舞狮表演的方法分露脚狮、基脚狮、高脚狮、矮脚狮等，舞狮表演既要注重形象的表现，又要生动传神，这是南狮艺术的精华。藤县舞狮的表演形式主要是采青和高桩表演。表演者通常二人合舞一个狮子，借助多种道具的设计展现出山、岭、岩、溪、涧、索、桥、水等大自然景物，通过在桩阵上跳跃腾飞等各种高难、惊险动作，表露狮子的喜、怒、醉、乐、醒、动、静、惊、疑、猛等神态，反映狮子历尽千辛万苦，克服重重困难、勇敢向前的精神及其最终获得的丰硕成果，从而把舞狮艺术推向拟人化的励志教育，将杂技、武术、技巧、舞蹈等技术融于狮艺之中，给观众以力与美的艺术享受。

The lion dance of Teng County belongs to the southern lion dance whose performing types include bare foot lion, base foot lion, high foot lion and short foot lion. The quintessence of southern lion dance lies in its focus on vivid expression of both the outside image and inside spirit. The main performing type of the lion dance of Teng County is Caiqing (Caiqing is a fixed action of lion dance which always push the dance to the climax)and high-stake. Two players usually cooperate to perform one lion and with the aid of the props, they present the natural scenery such as mountains, hills, rocks, streams, creeks, cable bridges and water. By way of various difficult and thrilling actions of jumping on the array of stakes, the players present the different images and expressions of the lion, including happiness, anger, drunkenness, joy, wake up, dynamic and static state, surprise, doubt, and fierce, which vividly reveals the lion's bravery over various difficulties and hardships and their eventual fruits, so as to prompt the personification of lion dance art into education and integrate acrobatics, martial arts, techniques and dance into lion dance, which provides the audience with the artistic enjoyment of strength and beauty.

등현사자춤은 남파사자춤에 속하며, 공연방법에는 노각사자, 기각사자, 골발사자, 조발사자 등이 있다. 사자춤은 형상적인 표현을 중시해야 할 뿐만 아니라 생동하고 생동하며, 이는 남사자예술의 정수이다. 등현사자춤의 공연형식은 주로 채록과 고막춤이다. 연기자들은 일반적으로 두 사람이 일치단결 한 사자 춤, 다양한 도구의 설계 산 령, 바위, 보 계, 간, 소 교, 물 등 자연 경 물, 말뚝 진지에서 점프로 도약하는 등 각종 고난도 액션, 사자의 표출 기쁨, 노여움, 취, 즐거움, 깨, 조용해, 놀라 서 어쩔 줄 모르고, 의심, 맹 등 태도, 반영 사자 천신만고 끝에, 온갖 어려움을 극복하고 용감하게 나아가는 정신과 최종적으로 얻은 풍성한 성과는 사자춤을 의인화된 교육으로 발전시키고 곡예, 무술, 기교, 무용 등 기술을 사자예술과 융합시켜 관중들에게 힘과 아름다움을 예술적으로 향수하게 한다.

舞狮活动是民间民俗文化的重要组成部分，有利于增进各民族之间的凝聚力，藤县狮舞不仅反映了藤县人民强烈的集体荣誉感和团结互助精神，也为传播中华民族优秀文化作出了不可磨灭的伟大贡献。

Lion dance is an important part of folk culture, which is conducive to enhancing the cohesion among all nationalities. The lion dance in Tengxian County not only reflects the strong sense of collective honor and spirit of solidarity and mutual assistance of the people of Tengxian County, but also makes great contribution to the spread of the excellent culture of the Chinese nation.

사자춤은 민간민속문화의 중요한 구성부분으로서 여러 민족간의 응집력을 증진시키는데 유리하다. 등현사자춤은 등현사람들의 강렬한 집단영예감과 단결협조의 정신을 반영하였을 뿐만 아니라 중화민족의 우수한 문화를 전파하는데 마멸할 수 없는 위대한 공헌을 하였다.

15. 田阳壮族狮舞

Lion Dance of Tianyang Zhuang Ethnic Group

[入选时间：2011　Time: 2011

遗产名录：第三批国家级非物质文化遗产扩展项目名录
Heritage Category: Extended list of the third batch of National Intangible Cultural Heritage.

地域：百色　Region: Baise]

田阳壮族舞狮流传于广西布洛陀文化发源地田阳，主要分布于田阳县河谷一带、坡洪镇及周边地区。田阳有着"舞狮之乡"的美称，逢年过节、五谷丰登、盛大活动等都以舞狮作乐。

Lion dance of Tianyang Zhuang lion dance is popular in Tianyang, the birthplace of Buluotuo culture in Guangxi. It is mainly distributed in the valley area of Tianyang County, Pohong Town and the surrounding areas. Tianyang has the reputation of "the town of lion dance", where lion dance will always be performed during festivals, harvest and grand celebration activities.

전양쫭족의 사자춤은 광시 포락타우문화의 발원지인 전양에서 전해지고 있으며, 주로 전양현 하곡일대, 포홍진 및 그 주변 지역에 분포되어 있다. 전양은 '사자춤의 고장'이라는 미칭을 가지고 있는데, 매년 명절이나 오곡이 풍만하고 성대한 행사 등에 모두 사자춤을 춘다.

田阳舞狮历史悠久，据史料记载，明朝嘉靖三十四年，壮民族英雄瓦氏夫人率田州假兵东征抗倭凯旋归来，田州民众纷纷组织盛大舞狮欢迎瓦氏以及士兵荣归故里。从此舞狮成为壮族文艺特有的表演节目，代代相传，久盛不衰。

Tianyang lion dance has a long history. According to the historical records, in the year 34 of Jiangqing Ming Dynasty, when Mrs. Wa, the Zhuang national hero, led her troops returning home in their triumph over the Japanese pirates, people in Tianzhou organized the grand lion dance to celebrate their return. From then on, lion dance has been a special artistic performance of Zhuang ethnic group from generation to generation.

전양사자춤의 역사는 유구하다. 명나라 가정 34년에 장족 영웅인 와씨부인이 전주의 위장병사를 거느리고 동정을 통해 왜구와의 전쟁에서 개선하여 돌아오자 전주의 민중들은 분분히 사자춤을 조직해 와씨와 병사들이 고향으로 돌아온 것을 환영했다고 한다. 이때로부터 사자춤은 쫭족문예의 특유의 공연레퍼토리로 되였으며 대대로 전해지면서 오래동안 성행하였다.

田阳壮族舞狮，有高难、惊险、奇美的特点，体现浓郁的民族特色。田阳壮族舞狮套路多，节目丰富，技术精湛，融武术、舞蹈、杂技于一体，有地面舞狮和高空舞狮两种表演形式。地面舞狮属文派舞狮，以活泼可爱的顽皮形象为特点，主要在地面表演闪、扑、挪、腾、滚或滑稽动作逗引人们，狮子由戴着顽皮马骝和满脸笑容的大头佛面具的队员一前一后带路引逗，在爆竹声和锣鼓打击乐的配合下表演，一般用于节日庆祝、拜年、祝贺、集会、婚庆、参军等活动；高空舞狮属武派舞狮，主要特点是把武术、杂技、舞蹈动作融进舞狮中，以高台表演为主，一般由一名手持狮珠的引狮者带路、逗引狮子表演各种扣人心弦的造型动作，可攀至20多张高凳叠起的金山上施展雄姿，或在半空高悬的钢索绳子上翻滚跳跃如履平地，还可在刀尖上表演顶肚旋转等。田阳壮族高空狮舞代表节目有《刀尖狮技》、《狮子上金山》、《狮子过天桥》、《高桩飞狮》和《金狮雄风》等。

Enjoying the characteristics of high difficulty, thrilling adventure and extraordinary beauty, The lion dance of Tianyang Zhuang ethnic group has rich patterns and superb skills, integrating martial arts, dance and acrobatics, and includes two types of performing, ground lion dance and high altitude lion dance. Ground lion dance belongs to the civil school, which is featured for lovely and cute images and amusing performances on the ground such as dodging, throwing, moving, jumping, rolling and other funny actions. Ground lion dance is usually performed in the activities of festival celebrations, New Year greetings, get-togethers, wedding ceremonies and army joining ceremonies, in which the lion is led by the players wearing cute monkey masks walking in the front and players wearing "big head Buddha" masks following in the back, with the accompany of firecrackers and drum and gong percussion performances. By way of contrast, high altitude lion dance belongs to military school, which is featured by integrating martial arts, acrobatics and dance movements into lion dance and mainly performed on the high platform. High altitude lion dance is usually performed by a lion leading player who holds a "lion pearl" teasing the lion to make all kinds of gripping actions such as presenting its handsome posture on the "Jinshan" (a pyramid structure piled up by more than 20 chairs), jumping on the mid-air wire rope as freely as on the ground, and spinning on the knife blade with belly on the top. The representative high altitude lion dance of Tianyang includes "lion dance on knife blade", "lion climbing Jinshan"," lion cross over the bridge", "flying lion on high stake", and "gold lion with glory posture".

전양장족의 사자춤은 어렵고 아찔하며 기이한 특징을 가지고 있어 짙은 민족 특색을 잘 보여준다. 전양장족의 사자춤은 공연이 풍부하고 기술이 정교하며 무술, 무용, 곡예를 일체화시켰으며 지상사자춤과 고공사자춤 두 가지 공연 형식이 있다. 바닥사자춤은 문파사자춤에 속하며 활발하고 귀여운 장난스러운 형상을 특색으로 주로 바닥에서 번쩍이고, 덮치고, 옮기고, 구르거나 익살스러운 동작을 하여 사람들을 웃긴다. 사자는 장난스러운 말갈기와 얼굴에 웃음을 띤 큰 머리의 불면구를 쓴 팀원들이 앞뒤에서 길을 안내하며 폭죽소리와 꽹과리, 북, 타악기의 배합하에 공연을 한다. 일반적으로 명절 경축, 새해 인사, 축하, 집회, 결혼, 입대 등 활동에 쓰인다. 고공사자춤은 무파사자춤에 속하는데 주요특징은 무술, 곡예, 무용동작을 사자춤에 융합시킨 것이며 높은 무대에서 공연하는 것을 위주로 한다. 보통 손에 사자구슬을 든 사자 안내자가 길을 인도하고 사자를 유혹하여 심금을 울리는 조형동작을 공연하는데, 20여 개의 높은 걸상이 겹쳐진 금산에 올라 웅대한 모습을 보이거나, 허공에 높이 걸려 있는 쇠줄 위에서 구르고 도약하며, 칼끝에서 배굴기 등 공연을 할 수도 있다. 전양장족 고공사자춤의 대표적인 프로그램으로는 「칼끝사자기술」, 「사자가 금산에 오르다」, 「사자가 구름다리를 건너다」, 「고두사자」,

「금사자웅풍」 등이 있다.

随着国家对优秀传统文化的重视与宣传，田阳舞狮队伍日益壮大，目前有田阳舞狮艺术团、秣马乐英舞狮队、坡洪舞狮队等16支舞狮团队和4支童狮队，每年表演多达200多场。

With the national emphasis on excellent traditional culture and publicity, Tianyang Lion dance team is growing day by day. At present, there are 16 lion dance teams such as Tianyang Lion Dance Art Troupe, Moma Leying Lion Dance Team, Pohong Lion Dance Team as well as 4 child lion teams, performing more than 200 performances every year.

국가에서 우수한 전통문화를 중시하고 선전함에 따라 전양사자춤팀은 날로 장성하여 현재 전양사자춤예술단, 말락영사자춤팀, 포홍사자춤팀 등 16개 사자춤팀과 4개 아동사자춤팀이 있으며 매년 200여 회에 걸쳐 공연을 하고 있다.

16. 铜鼓舞（南丹勤泽格拉）

Bronze Drum Dance (Chinzegra)

[入选时间：2014　Time: 2014

遗产名录：第四批国家级非物质文化遗产扩展项目名录

Heritage Category: Extended list of the fourth batch of National Intangible Cultural Heritage.

地域：河池　Region：Hechi]

"勤泽格拉"是白裤瑶语的音译，意为"打老猴"，是白裤瑶人民模仿自然界动物猴子的生活习性，把猴子形态引入舞蹈，又融合铜鼓伴奏而形成的，又称作"猴鼓舞"、"猴棍舞"或"铜鼓舞"。"勤泽格拉"是白裤瑶人民喜爱的传统舞蹈，是白裤瑶族人民在长期的社会发展过程中积淀的文化结晶，其内容蕴藏着白裤瑶历史、民俗、文化、信仰等诸多内涵，主要流行于在广西南丹县里湖、八圩两个瑶族乡的山寨里。

Chinzegra is translated from the language of Baiku Yao (a branch of Yao ethnic group in China, who gets its name for people wearing white trousers), meaning "play the monkey dance", which is formed by Yao people's long period of imitation of the monkey's life habits. It is accompanied by bronze drum, thus being called "monkey drum dance", "monkey stick dance" or "bronze drum dance". Being a traditional folk dance loved by the Baiku Yao people, Chinzegra is a cultural crystal accumulated in the long term of social development, and contains a rich connotation in Baiku Yao's history, folk custom, culture and belief. It is popular in Yao villages of Lihu and Baxu in Nandan County of Guangxi.

'친저그라'는 '늙은 원숭이를 때리다'라는 뜻의 흰바지요의 음역이다. 흰바지요 사람들이 자연계 동물인 원숭이의 생활 습성을 모방하여 원숭이 형태를 춤에 도입하고 또 동고 반주와 어울려서 만들어진 춤이다. '원숭이북춤', '원숭이막춤춤', '동북춤'이라고도 한다. '친저그라'는 흰바지요민(白裤瑶)이 좋아하는 전통무용이다. 흰바지요민(白裤瑶)이 장기적인 사회발전과정에서 축적한 문화의 결정체이다. 그 내용은 바이바지요의 역사, 민속, 문화, 신앙 등 많은 내용을 담고 있다.

勤泽格拉源自白裤瑶葬礼习俗，是为死去的亲人举办丧事时跳的一种祭祀性舞蹈，属于葬礼习俗中的铜鼓祭祀。勤泽格拉过程庄严且隆重，敲击鼓者均为男性，跳舞时将若干个铜鼓吊在木架上，一人左手拿锤打击铜鼓正中，右手拿一根小棒击打鼓边，另一人用一木桶反复送入或拉出鼓腔。若干面铜鼓被排列成门字形阵式，在这个周围挂着铜鼓的阵式中，有一个高约1米，直径约为60厘米的木鼓，一人在击木鼓的同时跳起舞蹈，这个击木鼓的舞蹈就是"勤泽格拉"。表演过程十分考究，击打位置讲究由从上到下，再由下到上的顺序，动作时而犹如猴子挠头抓脚，上蹿下跳，时而犹如农民在田间辛苦劳作。

Originating in the funeral customs of Baiku Yao ethnic group, Chinzegra is a sacrificial dance in the funeral ceremony and the bronze drum sacrifice in the the funeral customs. The process of Chinzegra is solemn and all played by males. During the sacrifice, several bronze drums are hung in the wooden racks. One player beats the center of the drum with the hammer in his left hand and beats the rim of the drum with a stick in his right hand, while the other player use a wooden barrel to frequently feed and pull out the drum. Bronze drums are arranged in an array of a door shape. In the center a player dances while beating the wooden drum which has a height of about 1 meter and a diameter of 60 centimeters, and this performance is called Chinzegra. The performance process is very elaborate with the beating positions performed in the order from top to bottom and then from bottom to top. Sometimes the movements are like monkeys scratching their heads and feet, jumping up and down, and sometimes they are like farmers working hard in the fields.

친지게라는 하얀바요장례풍속에서 기원하였는데 죽은 친족의 장례를 치를 때 추는 제사성무용으로 장례 풍속중의 동고(銅鼓) 제사에 속한다. 북치는 사람은 모두 남성이며 춤을 출 때 여러 개의 동고를 나무틀에 매달아 놓고 한 사람은 왼손으로 망치로 동고 가운데를 치고 오른손으로 작은 막대기로 북끝을 치며 다른 한 사람은 나무통을 이용해 반복적으로 북가락을 넣거나 당긴다. 여러 개의 동고가 문자형으로 늘어서 있고, 그 주변에 동고가 매달려 있는 가운데 높이 1m, 지름 60cm 정도의 목고가 있다. 이 목고를 치면서 한 사람이 춤을 추는 이 춤이 친저글라다. 공연과정에 아주 주의를 돌리며 타격위치가 우에서 아래로, 다시 아래로부터 우로 순서를 따지며 동작은 원숭이가 머리를 긁고 발을 긁는 것 같기도 하고 우에서 뛰어내리는 것 같기도 하며 밭에서 힘들게 일하는 것 같기도 하다.

勤泽格拉在音乐节奏、舞蹈姿态都有其独特之处，且在 不同场景中以其独特魅力表达着不同的寓意和功能，丧葬仪式过程为先人执绋，以表哀思，在年街节中勤泽格拉又成了愉悦的欢庆方式。勤泽格拉这一传统民俗体育项目，已不再仅是简单的艺术形态，更是白裤瑶族祭祀先祖、典庆仪式中不可替代的关键组成，是瑶族文化的一个重要组成部份，是瑶族民族精神文化的表现形式，堪称"白裤瑶文明发展的 活化石"。

Chinzegra has its unique musical rhythm and dance gestures, and conveys different meanings and functions in different Settings. In funeral ceremonies it is performed to express mourning for the deceased, while in the Annual Street festivals it is selected in the form of a joyful celebration. Chinzegra, a traditional folk sport, is no longer just a simple artistic form, but also an irreplaceable key component in the sacrificial rites and celebration ceremonies of Baiku Yao people. As an important part of the Yao culture and the expression form of the their spiritual culture, Chinzegra is regarded as "the living fossil of the development of the Baiku Yao civilization".

진저겔라는 음악 리듬과 춤에서 독특한 점을 갖고 있다. 또한 장면마다 독특한 매력으로 다양한 의미와 기능을 표현한다. 장례식 과정에서 고인의 동아줄을 잡고 애도의 뜻을 표현하며, 춘절 거리축제에서도 진저겔라는 즐거운 축제의 수단이 된다. 친저게라는이 전통 민속 체육 종목은 더 이상 단순한 예술 형태가 아니라 요족 선조에게 제사를 지내고 요족의 경축 의식에서 대체할 수 없는 관건적인 구성으로 요족 문화의 중요한 구성 부분이자 요족 정신문화의 표현형식으로서 '바이지야오 문명 발전의 산화석'이라고 할 만하다.

17. 瑶族金锣舞

Jinluo Dance of Yao Ethnic Group

[入选时间：2014　Time: 2014

遗产名录：第四批国家级非物质文化遗产名录

Heritage Category: List of the fourth batch of National Intangible Cultural Heritage.

地域：百色　Region: Baise]

金锣舞流行于广西田东县作登瑶族乡梅林、平略等村，是田东境内布努瑶民族民间舞蹈的一个代表性作品。

Jinluo (gold gongs) dance is popular in Meilin, Pinglue Villages of Zuodeng Yao-populated Township in Tiandong County, Guangxi and it is a representative work of Bunu Yao folk dance in Tiandong County.

금징춤은 광시 전동(田东) 현 작등요족 (作登瑶族) 향 메이린(梅林), 핑요(平略) 등 마을에서 유행된 것으로 전동 경내의 부누요(布努瑶) 민족 민간무용의 대표적인 작품이다.

金锣舞是瑶人民在长期劳动过程中创造出的具有浓郁民族特征和独特艺术形式的民间传统舞蹈，起初只限用于酬神、祭祀、驱邪等民俗活动，后来演变为贺新春、庆丰年的主要舞蹈。每年的春节和农历五月廿九，金锣声就会在瑶寨响起，人们如痴如狂唱歌跳舞。金锣舞是瑶民情感渲泻的主要活动形式，体现了当地瑶民的生产、生活、情感的全过程。

It is a traditional folk dance with strong national characteristics and unique art forms, created Yao people during their long process of laboring. At first, it was only served as paying tribute to the Gods, offering sacrifices, driving away evils and other folk activities. Later it turned into the main dance for people's celebrating Spring Festival and harvests. Every year on Spring

Festival and the 29th of the 5th lunar month, the sound of gold gongs will ring in the Yao village and attracts people to sing and dance to their hearts. Jinluo dance is a major way for Yao people to express their emotion and thus, reveals the whole process of working, life and emotion of the local Yao people.

금징무용은 요나라 인민들이 장기적인 로동과정에서 창조해 낸 짙은 민족특징과 독특한 예술형식을 갖춘 민간전통무용이다. 매년 설날과 음력 5월 29일 요촌에서는 징소리가 울려 퍼지며 사람들은 미친 듯이 노래하고 춤을 춘다. 금징춤은 요민 (瑶民)의 감정이 흘러내리는 주요 활동 형식으로서 현지 요민의 생산, 생활, 감정의 전 과정을 구현하였다.

瑶族的习俗是用玉米供养着金锣，一年四季将金锣用玉米埋起来，"养在"在粮仓里。每年大年三十，瑶民们提前从粮仓里取出金锣。然后将其放到堂屋中间的神台上，一边祭拜一边说"金锣金锣一年365天，到今晚一年就过去了，今晚我们特地请您出来和我们一起吃年饭，首先请您先吃，您吃完后，您就在旁边等我们，家里面吃完年夜饭后，您就来和我们一起跳金锣舞"。祈祷完后就将三杯酒洒到方桌前，然后把金锣放到神台上，撤下方桌，全家才"享受金锣恩赐的美食"。年夜饭后，将金锣悬挂在堂屋的中间，全家人围住金锣敲锣起舞，直到天亮。大年初一，全家老少穿上新装，瑶胞们相互串门，每到一户人家都要唱起瑶歌，跳起金锣舞。这样的活动一直持续到二月初一封锣为止。

It is Yao people's custom to keep the golden gong with corn in a granary throughout the year. Every year on Chinese New Year's Eve, the Yao people take out the gold gongs from their granaries and place it on the altar which is in the middle of the hall. During worship they would cite "gold gong, gold gong, 365 days a year, tonight comes to the end, tonight we sincerely ask you to come out and have dinner with us, you enjoy it first, after you eat, please wait for us, when we all finish, we invite you to dance together." After the prayer, three glasses of wine are poured on the square table, and the gold gong is placed on the altar. The square table is removed, and the whole family would enjoy the delicious food blessed by the gold gong. After the New Year's Eve dinner, the gold gong is hung in the middle of the room and the whole family dance around it until dawn. On the first day of the Lunar New Year, the whole family, young and old, put on their new clothes to visit each other and sing Yao songs and perform Jinluo dance. This practice continues until the beginning of February in lunar month.

요족은 옥수수로 징을 공양하고, 일년 사계절 징을 옥수수에 묻혀 곡창에 '기른다'. 매년 섣달 그믐날이 되면 요민들은 미리 곡창에서 징을 꺼낸다. 그리고 몸 채의 중간에 있는데, 제사하면서 말'울리다 울리다 1년 365일, 오늘 저녁까지 1년이 지나갔고 오늘 밤 우리는 특히 당신이 나와서 우리와 함께 먹 적지 않은 우선 먼저 드세요 먹고 후에 당신은 바로

옆에서 우리를 기다리고, 집 안에 음식을 먹고 난 후에 당신이 오 우리와 함께 울리다 춤을 추게 했다. "기도를 마친 뒤 술 석 잔을 네모상 앞에 뿌리고, 징을 신대에 올려 상을 치워야" 온 가족이 '징을 즐긴다'. 제야(除夜) 식사가 끝나면 금징을 당방 가운데에 매달고 온 가족이 금징을 둘러싸고 춤을 추면서 날이 밝을 때까지 징을 친다. 정월 초하루이면 온 가족이 새 옷을 입고 요네 동포들이 집집마다 요가를 부르고 금과춤을 춘다. 이런 행사가 2월 초 첫 행사가 열릴 때까지 이어졌다.

金锣舞多以集体舞为主，人数可为三、五人，也可几百上千。跳舞时在活动场地中拉起一条藤蔓或一根绳索，把金锣串起并悬挂起来，也可将金锣吊于竹架或木杈上，离地面约一米五左右。由于瑶族多居住在高山上，长期在山地生活、劳动使他们为了适应自然环境养成了在崎岖山路行走时，必须抬高脚步，脚尖用力，以及腰部扭摆并含胸等习惯，金锣舞动作里的"抬腿击锣"、"靠步点锣"、"双槌过头"、"双槌背击"、"急转点锣"等就是这些习惯的体现，狂放的金锣舞让人看到了生命的张力和艺术的美。

Jinluo dance is majorly a group dance, in which the number of the dancers varies from three or five people to more than hundreds or thousands. When performing the dance, the gold gong will be hung 1.5 meters above the ground on a piece of vine or rope which is put in the center of the yard or on the bamboo rack or wood branch. Yao people mostly inhabited in high mountains, and under long period of living and working on the high mountain they had formed some habits to adapt to the natural environment, such as raising footsteps, putting force in tiptoes, twisting waists and lowering chest while walking on the rugged mountain roads. These habits of Yao people could be found in the movements of Jinluo dance, such as striking the gong with leg lifting, touching the gong with stepping, dancing with two hammers overhead, dancing with two hammers striking at the back, touching the gong with sharp turn. The wild Jinluo dance exposes the tension of life and the beauty of art.

징무는 대부분 집단무를 위주로 하며, 인원수는 3, 5명이 될 수도 있고, 몇 백, 수천 명이 될 수도 있다. 춤을 출 때 행사장에서 덩굴이나 밧줄을 당겨 금징을 매달아 매달거나 대나무기둥이나 나무가지에 매달 수 있는데 지면에서 약 1.5m 떨어져 있다. 요족은 대부분 높은 산에서 생활하였기에 장기적으로 산간지대에서 생활하고 일하면서 자연환경에 적응하기 위하여 험한 산길을 걸을 때에는 반드시 걸음을 높이 들고 발끝에 힘을 주며 허리를 비틀고 가슴을 찌르는 등 습관을 길렀다. 금과무용 동작에서 다리를 들어 꽹과리 치기, 스텝에 의지해 꽹과리 찍기, 쌍두리 머리, 쌍두리 등 치기, 급전 점징 등이 바로 이런 관습의 체현이다. 폭주하는 금과리무는 사람들에게 생명의 장력과 예술의 아름다움을 보게 한다.

在瑶民心中，金锣是一种神物，一种精神信仰，这种信仰文化的流传是自觉的、长久的。如今，金锣舞不仅是村民的一种文化娱乐项目，还成了重大节庆活动必不可少的保留节目。是瑶族人民喜爱的民族舞蹈，更是瑶族的优秀传统文化。

Gold gong is a divine object and a spiritual belief in the eyes of Yao people. The spread of this culture belief is conscious and long-lasting. Nowadays, Jinluo dance is not only a cultural entertainment for villagers, but also an essential part of major festivals. It is a favorite national dance and an excellent traditional culture of the Yao people.

요민 (瑤民)의 마음에 금징은 일종의 신물(神物) 이자 정신적 신앙으로, 이러한 신앙문화는 자각적으로, 장기적으로 전해진다. 오늘날 금징춤은 촌민들의 문화오락종목일 뿐만 아니라 중대한 경축행사에서 없어서는 안될 보존종목으로 되였다. 이는 요족인민이 즐기는 민족무용이며 더우기는 요족의 우수한 전통문화이다.

18. 京族哈节

Ha Festival of Jing Ethnic Group

[入选时间：2006 Time: 2006
遗产名录：第一批国家级非物质文化遗产名录
Heritage Category: List of the first batch of National Intangible Cultural Heritage.
地域：防城港 Region: Fangchenggang]

哈节是京族最隆重的传统节日，哈节文化主要分布于京族聚居的广西东兴市江平镇的巫头、山心、万尾三个岛屿（俗称"京族三岛"）及其附近的村屯。

Ha Festival is the grandest traditional festival of Jing ethnic group, and its culture is mainly popular across the three Jing-populated islands of Wutou, Shanxin, Wanwei (commonly known as the "three islands of Jing ethnic group") and the villages nearby in Jiangping Town of Dongxing City Guangxi.

하 축제는 징족의 가장 성대한 전통 명절이다. 하 축제 문화는 주로 징족이 모여 사는 광시 둥싱시 장핑진의 우터우, 산심, 완웨이 세 섬 (속칭 '징족 3섬')과 그 부근의 마을에 분포되어 있다.

关于哈节有不少民间传说，其中比较有代表性的传说称：古代有位歌仙来到京族三岛，以传歌为名，动员群众起来反抗封建压迫。她的歌声感动了许多群众。后人为了纪念她，建立了"哈亭"，定期在哈亭唱歌传歌，渐成节俗，就成了京族人一年一度的传统节日哈节，各村的哈亭也就成了节日活动的中心。

There are many folk legends about the Ha Festival, among which the more representative one has it that in ancient time a Song Fairy came to the three Jing-populated islands and persuaded people to fight against feudal oppression in the name of singing. People were touched by her song and later generations built the "Ha pavilion" in order to commemorate her. The regular singing activity in Ha pavilion gradually formed into the traditional Ha Festival celebrated yearly by Jing people and making the Ha pavilion the center of the festival activities.

하 축제에 관한 민간전설은 적지 않은데 그중에서 비교적 대표적인 전설은 고대에 한 가선이 징족 3섬에 와서 노래를 전한다는 명의로 군중을 동원하여 봉건적압박에 반항하게 하였다고 한다. 그녀의 노랫소리는 많은 군중을 감동시켰다. 후세 사람들은 그녀를 기념하기 위해 '하팅 (哈亭)'을 세우고 정기적으로 이곳에서 노래를 부르면서 노래를 전했는데 점차 명절 풍속으로 바뀌어 1년에 한 번 열리는 징족의 전통 명절인 '하팅 (哈亭) 축제'가 되었고, 각 마을의 하팅은 명절 활동의 중심이 되었다.

在长期的生产生活过程中，京族虽然受到了汉族、壮族等民族文化的影响，但其传统节日哈节却仍一直保持着海洋民族的特点，近五百年来连续不断，在不同的地区庆祝日期略有差异：万尾、巫头两岛是在农历六月初十，山心岛在农历八月初十，红坎村则在农历正月十五。虽日期各异，但节日的形式与内容基本相同。

In the process of long-term working and living, Jing ethnic group had been influenced by the culture of Han, Zhuang and other ethnic groups. However, its traditional Ha Festival has kept the feature of Oceanic group and lasted for nearly 500 years despite some differences in celebration dates: two islands of Wanwei and Wutou celebrating on the 10th of the sixth lunar month, 10th of the eighth lunar month in Shanxin island, and 15th of the first lunar month in Hongkan Village. Although the dates varies, the form and content of the festival stays basically the same.

장기간의 생산과 생활 과정에서 징 족은 한족, 쫭 족 등 민족문화의 영향을 받았는데도 그 전통 명절 아르 절 해양 민족의 특 점을 계속하면서 최근 5년 동안 계속해서, 다른 지역에서 축하 날짜의 차이만 꼬리, 무당 머리 두 섬은 음력 6월 초 열흘, 산 가슴이 섬에서 음력 8월 초 열흘 붉은 칸 촌은 음력 정월 대보름. 비록 날짜가 각기 다르지만 명절의 형식과 내용은 기본적으로 같다.

哈节庆典活动一般持续一周左右，大体分为迎神、祭神、坐蒙（入席）、送神四个部分。迎神在哈节的第一天，村民齐集哈亭，等到吉时便集队举旗擎伞，抬着神架到海边迎神，把神仙迎回哈亭供奉。祭神分为大祭和小祭，哈节第二天是大祭，随后几天都是小祭，祭神仪式一般从上午11点开始，约持续两个小时。坐蒙在哈节的后两天进行，祭神完毕后，在哈亭内设席饮宴和听歌，宴席中盛放菜肴的长方形木托盘在京族中称为"蒙"，所以乡饮、听哈称为"坐蒙"，按传统规定，凡本地京族男子，到了18岁便有资格入席，入席须以族长、长老为首，按照辈分就坐。宴席中有哈妹"唱哈"独弦琴表演等独具京族特色的文娱表演。送神要等到哈节最后一天的吉时，香公在神位前念颂《送神词》，哈妹们跳起"花灯舞"，将神灵平安送走。

Generally Ha Festival celebrations last about a week and can be divided into four parts, namely, greeting god, worship god, Zuomeng (being seated), sending god. Greeting god happens on the first day of Ha Festival, on which the villagers assemble in Ha pavilion, and they would not start carrying the god seat for the seaside with flags and umbrellas on until the auspicious time comes. They carry the god back to Ha pavilion for sacrifice. The worship part includes Big sacrifice and small sacrifice. The second day of Ha Festival is Big sacrifice and followed by a few days of small sacrifice, on which the ritual usually starts at 11 o'clock in the morning and lasts for two hours. Zuomeng happens on the last two days of Ha Festival when the worship finishes a feast is set for people to listen to *Ha* (literally translates as song in their local language). Since the rectangular wooden tray used in the feast is called "meng" in Jing language, listening to Ha while drinking is named as "zuomeng". According to the customs, every male local Jing man, aged over 18 years old is eligible to sit at the table, but they have to sit by generations with chief and group leader first. During the feast, there are entertainment performances with unique Jing characteristics, such as singing by Ha girls and single-string fiddle performance. Sending god needs to wait until the auspicious time on the last day of Ha Festival, at which the Xianggong (the person who resides the sending god ritual) reads the eulogy of "sending god" in front of the memorial tablet and the Ha girls dance "lantern dance" to send the god away safely.

하 축제는 보통 1주일 정도 진행되며, 크게 영신, 제신, 좌몽(자리), 송신 네 부분으로 나뉜다. 영신절 첫날에 마을 사람들은 모두 합정에 모여 길가가 되면 대오를 모아 기와 우산을 들고 신받침대를 들고 해변에 나가 신을 마중하고 신선을 합정에 모시고 간다. 제사는 대제와 소제로 나뉘는데 합절 다음날은 대제이고 그 다음 며칠은 소제이다. 제사는 보통 오전 11시에 시작하여 약 2시간 동안 진행된다. 우에 앉아 절 한 이틀 후, 제사가 끝나면서 헤 정이 석 연회와 들 헤, 연회석에서 반찬을 담는 장방형의 나무는 트 레이 징 족에서 '몽'이라고 한다. 그래서 향 ·하 '앉아 몽'이라고 듣고 마시는 전통적인 규정에 따라 모든 로컬 징 족 남자, 18세가 되면 자격이 있는 자리에 앉아 주십시오, 자리에 반드시 족장, 장로를 비롯해 항렬대로 착석하였다. 연회석에는 하매(哈妹)의 '하하노래' 독현악기 공연 등 징족 특유의 문화 오락 공연이 있었다. 송신하는 하절의 마지막 날인 길시, 향공이 신위 앞에서 '송신사'를 낭독하면 하매들은 '화등춤'을 추며 신령을 무사히 보낸다.

京族哈节丰富的内涵和古朴的风格生动地展示了京族悠久的历史、独特的生活习俗以及京族多姿多彩的文化风貌，是京族传统文化的集中体现。

The rich connotation and simple style of Ha Festival vividly reveal the long history and unique living customs as well as the colorful cultural styles of Jing ethnic group, which is also the embodiment of the traditional culture of Jing ethnic group.

징족 하 축제의 풍부한 내용과 고박한 풍격은 징족의 유구한 역사, 독특한 생활풍습 및 다채로운 문화풍격을 생동하게 보여주고 있으며 징족의 전통문화를 집중적으로 보여주고 있다.

19. 毛南族肥套

Feitao of Maonan Ethnic Group

[入选时间：2006 Time: 2006

遗产名录：第一批国家级非物质文化遗产名录

Heritage Category: List of the first batch of National Intangible Cultural Heritage.

地域： 河池　　Region: Hechi]

"肥套"是毛南语，汉语译为"还愿""傩戏"，是毛南族还愿等活动的总称。"肥"在毛南语中意为"做、举办、举行"等，"套"意即含有说唱、朗诵、舞蹈等祈神成分的综合仪式。

Feitao is Maonan language, translated as "Nuo drama" and "Wish returning" in Chinese. It is the general name of Maonan people's Returning Wish (vow-repaying) Activities. "Fei" in Maonan language means "do and hold", while "Tao" is a comprehensive ceremony containing rap, recitation, dance and other praying practices.

'페이타오'는 마오난어로 중국어로는 '소원갚기', '나희'로 번역되는데, 마오난족이 소원갚기 등 활동에 대한 총칭이다. '비'는 마오난어로'하다·거행하다·거행하다' 등을 뜻하고, '투'는 설창·낭송·춤 등 기신 요소가 포함된 의식을 뜻한다.

毛南族肥套流传于广西环江毛南族自治县西南部的下南乡。盛行于明清之际，初为毛南族借助傩祭祀天地自然万物的仪式，在传承过程中融合毛南族口头文学、山歌、戏剧、舞蹈、音乐、打击乐等艺术元素成为内容丰富的民俗活动。

Feitao of Maonan Ethnic Group is popular in the Xianan Township which is located in the southwest of Huanjiang Maonan Autonomous County of Guangxi. It prevailed in Ming and Qing Dynasties. At the beginning, Maonan people used

Nuo rituals to sacrifice the heavens and the earth, while in the process of inheritance, they integrated Maonan oral literature, folk songs, drama, dance, music, percussion music and other artistic elements into rich folk activities.

모남족비료는 광서 환강모남족자치현 서남부의 하남향에 유전되었다. 명, 청 시기에 성행하였는데 처음에는 모난족이 나오를 빌어 천지자연만물을 제사지내는 의식이였는데 전승과정에서 모난족 구전문학, 산가, 연극, 무용, 음악, 타악 등 예술요소가 융합되어, 내용이 풍부한 민속활동이 되었다.

毛南族肥套种类繁多，内容丰富，其主要表现形式有傩歌、傩舞、傩乐、傩故事（口头传说）、傩面具雕刻几大类。"肥套"共有十几个舞蹈场面。"还愿"时需要摆设各种"供桌"，搭神坛，挂神像，舞蹈活动均用一班师公主持进行。表演由一帮专业的神职人员主持，整体结构由十五个舞蹈组成，内容非常丰富，包括登梯、超度、架桥、拣花、送花、坐殿等。舞蹈的基本动作有软拜步、起伏碎步、甩袖、绕手轻拜、跳小步和辗转绕圈等，很少有剧烈的跳蹦。动作规律是在流动行进中起伏跳荡，轻柔悠然，气氛较为庄重肃穆。男性神多身穿龙袍、蟒袍，袍上绣着各种鲜艳的图形，并配上闪光片。女性神则上衫下裤，不穿裙，与民间妇女的服饰大致相同。

Feitao is rich in form and content, which are mainly manifested in Nuo song, Nuo dance, Nuo music, Nuo story (oral legend) and Nuo mask carving. There are more than a dozen dancing scenes in Maonan Feitao. In the scene of Wish Returning, various" *tables*" and altars needed to be set up, God paintings to be hung up and dancing activities to be presided by Shigong (folk masters). The performance is presided by a group of ritual men, with the overall structure consisting 15 dances of rich contents, including ladder climbing, soul releasing, bridge setting, flower picking, flower sending and hall sitting. The basic movements of the dance include gentle worship step, fluctuating quick and short step, sleeve swinging, hand-twisting light worship, jumping small steps and tossing and turning in circles, among which wild movements are rarely seen. The pattern of the dance is usually rising and falling while flowing forward, gently and leisurely, and the atmosphere is usually solemn. Actors playing male god wear dragon ropes and boa ropes, which are embroidered with patterns in bright colors and decorated with sequins, while actors playing female god wear top garment and trousers, no skirt, which is roughly the same as that of the folk woman.

모난족 비료세트는 종류가 많고 내용이 풍부하며, 그 주요 표현형식은 나가 · 나무 · 나악 · 나이야기(구두전설) · 나면조각 등 몇 가지 큰 종류가 있다." "모두 10여개 무용장면이 있다.", "약속이행"을 할 때에는 각종 "제상"을 차리고 신단을 설치하고 신상을 걸며 무용활동을 진행하는데 모두 스승의 주최하에 진행한다. 공연은 전문 성직자들이 주관하고 전체 구조는 15개의 무용으로 구성되었으며 내용이 매우 풍부한데, 사다리에 오르기, 천도(天道), 다리 가설, 꽃주우기, 꽃선물, 좌전(左殿) 등이 포함된다. 무용의 기본동작은 부드러운 스텝과 종종걸음,

소매흔들기, 가벼운 손돌리기, 작은 스텝과 원 돌리기 등이다. 격렬한 뜀놀이는 드물다. 동작법칙은 류동과정에 기복하고 요동치며 가볍고 유연하며 분위기가 비교적 장중하고 엄숙하다. 남성신들은 대부분 용포(龍袍)나 보아포(보아포)를 입고 있는데, 그것에는 화려한 도형과 섬광이 새겨져 있다. 여성신은 웃옷과 아래옷을 입고 치마를 입지 않는데 민간여성들의 복식과 대체로 같다.

毛南族肥套傩俗历经无数个历史朝代顽强的存活下来，发展和演变，反映着毛南族社会发展的历史。傩俗歌、舞、乐、戏多种娱乐形式也承载着毛南人祈求民族生生不息、冀望来年风调雨顺、五谷丰登的美好愿望，透射出毛南族文化艺术与其他民族文化艺术的融合与嬗变，既是毛南族发展的历史见证，又是毛南族传统文化的珍贵遗产。

Nuo customs of Maonan Feitao survived and developed through many historical dynasties, reflecting the history of Maonan social development. Various entertainment forms of Nuo song, dance, music and drama carry Maonan people's wishes for thriving nation, and good harvest for the next year, as well as reflect the fusion and transformation of Maonan national culture and art with other national culture and art. It is not only a historical testimony of Maonan development, but also a precious heritage of Maonan traditional culture.

모남족의 비투나속은 수많은 역사조대를 거치면서 완강하게 생존하고 발전, 변천하였는데 이는 모남족사회발전의 역사를 반영하고 있다. 나속가, 춤, 악, 극 등 여러가지 오락형식에는 민족이 영원히 번영하기를 기원하고 내년에 날씨가 좋으며 오곡이 풍족하기를 바라는 마오난 사람들의 아름다운 염원이 담겨져 있다. 이는 모난족의 문화예술과 기타 민족 문화예술의 융합과 변천과정을 보여주고 있으며 모난족의 발전을 보여주는 역사적 증인일 뿐만 아니라 모난족 전통문화의 귀중한 유산이기도 하다.

20. 瑶族盘王节

Panwang Festival of Yao Ethnic Group
[入选时间：2006　Time: 2006
遗产名录：第一批国家级非物质文化遗产名录
Heritage Category: List of the first batch of National Intangible Cultural Heritage.
地域：　贺州　　Region:　Hezhou]

瑶族盘王节，又称"盘王愿""跳盘王""踏歌堂""朝踏节"，是瑶族祭祀祖先盘王（盘瓠）的盛大节日，迄今已有1700多年历史。由分布在广西、广东、贵州、云南、湖南等地的盘氏家族发起的盘王节已成为全国盘王节祭祀最盛大的节日。广西的瑶族盘王节活动流行于广西的富川、钟山、八步、恭城、金秀等地区。

Panwang(King of Pan) Festival of Yao Ethnic Group, also called "Panwang Wish", "Dance about Panwang"," Tage Hall"," Chaota Festival" is a grand festival that Yao people worship their ancestors (Panhu) over a history of 1,700 years. The Panwang festival initiated by Pan family from Guangxi, Guangdong, Guizhou, Yunnan, Hunan has become the most grantest one around China. This Festival in Guangxi is popular in regions such as Fuchuan, Zhongshan, Babu, Gongcheng, Jinxiu.

Note: Tage: singing accompanied by stamping of feet or rhythmic dancing peculiar to Miao and Yao ethnic groups.
Chaota: Chaota means starting with rising sun. Chaota Festival presents the hardship of Yao ethnic group's ancestors by means of dancing and singing.

요족반왕절은 '반왕원', '점반왕', '답당', '조답절'이라고도 하는데 요족이 조상 반왕(반속)에게 제사를 지내는 성대한 명절로서 지금까지 1700여 년의 역사를 가지고 있다. 광시(广西) · 광동(廣東) · 귀주(貴州) ·

운남(雲南) · 호남(湖南) 등지에 분포한 반씨(版氏) 문중에서 발기된 반왕제는 이미 전국 반왕제 제사 중에서 가장 성대한 명절이 되었다. 광시의 요족반왕절 행사는 광시의 부천 · 종산 · 팔보 · 공성 · 금수 등 지역에서 유행하였다.

各地瑶族过盘王节的时间不一致，一般在秋收后至春节前的农闲时间举行，分定期和不定期两种，限期包括三天两夜和七天七夜两种。1984年8月，全国瑶族代表座谈会在广西南宁召开，确定每年农历十月十六日为瑶族的统一节日"盘王节"。在盘王节上瑶族男女老少都穿上节日盛装，用吟唱、祭酒、舞蹈、上香等形式来祭祀盘王先祖，追溯历史。唱歌跳舞，祈求全族平安顺利，来年风调雨顺，五谷丰收的传统节日。

People in different regions celebrate Panwang Festival in different times. Generally, it is held, regularly and irregularly, during the slack time from autumn harvest to Spring Festival. And it lasts for three days and two nights and seven days and seven nights respectively. In August 1984, a symposium of representatives of the Yao ethnic group was held in Nanning, Guangxi. It was determined that the 16th of the 10th lunar month of each year was the "Panwang Festival" of the Yao ethnic group. On Panwang Festival, people of Yao ethnic group, man and woman, old and young, all dress in their festival costumes, offer sacrifices to their ancestor of Panwang and memorizes their history in the forms of singing, offering wine, dancing and offering incense. By singing and dancing, they pray for peace, prosperity and good harvest for the whole group in the coming year.

각지의 요족들이 반왕절을 지내는 시간은 일치하지 않았는데 일반적으로 추수후부터 음력설전의 농한기에 거행하였는데 정기적, 비정기적 두가지로 나뉘었고 기한부에는 2 박 3일과 7 박 7일 두 가지가 있었다. 1984년 8월, 전국 요족대표 좌담회가 광시 남녕에서 개최되어 매년 음력 10월 16일을 요족의 통일명절인 '반왕절'로 정했다. 반왕절에 요족(瑶族)의 남녀노소는 모두 명절 옷을 입고 읊조리고, 술에 제를 지내고, 춤을 추고, 향을 올리는 등의 형식으로 반왕의 선조에게 제사를 지내며 역사를 거슬러 올라간다. 노래하고 춤추며 온 가족이 평안하고 순조로우며 내년에는 날씨가 좋고 오곡이 풍작을 거두기를 기원하는 전통 명절이다.

瑶族盘王节有相对固定的程序，主要包括三大部分：敬盘王、唱盘王和跳盘王。敬盘王就是设置祭坛、悬挂神像敬奉盘王；唱盘王就是唱盘王歌，吟唱表现瑶族神话、历史、政治、经济、文化艺术、社会生活等内容的历史长诗《盘王大歌》；跳盘王是跳盘王舞，以鼓锣伴奏，时而有男女伴唱，动作健美威武，再现了瑶族先民耕种狩猎，出征杀敌的画面。

Panwang Festival of Yao has a relatively fixed procedure, which mainly includes three parts, worshiping Panwang, reciting Panwang and dancing Panwang. Worshiping Panwang is to set up altars and hang gods portraits to sacrifice; Reciting PanWang is to sing a long historical poem "Pan Wang Grand song", which expresses the myth, history, politics, economy, cultural art, and social life of the Yao people. Panwang dance is accompanied by drums and gongs and sometimes accompanied by male and female singers. The movements are fit and powerful, reproducing the pictures of the Yao ancestors farming, hunting, and going out to fight and kill the enemies.

요족의 반왕절은 상대적으로 고정된 순서(순서)가 있으며 주로 경반왕(敬盘王), 창반왕(唱盘王), 도반왕(跳盘王) 등 세 부분으로 구성된다. "경반왕"이란 제단을 설치하고 신상을 걸어 "경반왕"을 섬기는 것이다. 반왕가를 부르는 것은 요족의 신화, 역사, 정치, 경제, 문화예술, 사회생활 등의 내용을 담은 장편시「반왕대가」를 부르는 것이다. 반왕춤은 반왕무를 말하는데 북과 꽹과리를 반주하고 때로는 남녀가 함께 노래를 부르는데 동작은 건강하고 위풍당당하여 요족 선민들이 농사를 짓고 수렵을 하며 출정하여 적을 무리는 모습을 재현하였다.

盘王节仪式由4名正师公主持，各司其职，还愿师、祭兵师、赏兵师、五谷师，每人1名助手，共8人，此外还有4名歌娘歌师、6名童男童女、1名长鼓艺人和唢呐乐队参与盘王节。

The ceremony of Panwang Festival is held by four arch masters, each performing his or her own duties. Masters in charge of redeeming wish, sacrificing, rewarding and grain praying are aided by one assistant respectively. In addition, four female singers, six young boys and girls, one long drum musician and a Suona horn band also involved in the festival.

반왕절 의식은 4명의 정사공 (正師公)이 주관하고, 각자 맡은 바 일을 하며, 환원사, 제병사, 상병사, 오곡사, 각 1명의 조수 등 모두 8명으로 구성된다. 이외에 가랑가사 4명, 소년동녀 6명, 장구 예인 1명과 수르나이 악단이 반왕절에 참여한다.

盘王节作为历史悠久、分布广泛的大众节庆活动，集瑶族传统文化之大成，是一种增强民族向心力、维系民族团结的人文盛典。

As a popular festival with a long history and wide distribution, Panwang Festival is a grand cultural ceremony which is conducive to strengthen the national centripetal force and maintain national unity.

반왕절은 역사가 유구하고 분포가 광범위한 대중 축제로서 요족 전통문화를 집대성하여 민족의 구심력을 강화하고 민족의 단결을 유지하는 인문성대한 행사이다.

21. 壮族歌圩

Song Fair of Zhuang Ethnic Group
[入选时间: 2006 Time: 2006
遗产名录: 第一批国家级非物质文化遗产名录
Heritage Category: List of the first batch of National Intangible Cultural Heritage.
地域: 南宁　Region: Nanning]

"歌圩"是壮族群众在特定时间、地点举行的节日性聚会歌唱活动形式，壮语称为"圩欢""圩逢""笼峒""窝坡"等。它是壮族民间传统文化活动的，也是男女青年进行社交的场所。

Song Fair is a form of festival gathering and singing activity held by Zhuang people at a specific time and place. It is called "Xu Huan", "Xu Feng", "Long Dong" and "Wo Po" in Zhuang languages. As a traditional folk cultural activity of Zhuang Ethnic Group, it is also the social gathering place for the youth.

가우는 쫭족 군중들이 특정 시간과 장소에서 거행하는 명절성 모임과 노래 활동 형식으로 쫭어로는 '허환', '허펑', '롱둥', '와파' 등으로 불린다. 이곳은 쫭족민간 전통문화활동의 장소이며 남녀청년들이 사교를 진행하는 장소이기도 하다.

歌圩源于氏族部落时代祭祀性的歌舞活动，随着社会的发展，这种原始仪式性的群体歌舞由"娱神"向"娱人"过渡，从"舞化"朝"歌化"发展，从而形成群体性酬唱的歌圩活动。壮族歌圩，在长期发展的过程中有着许多动人的传说，如祷祝丰年、赛歌择婿、歌仙刘三姐传歌等。其中比较流行的是"赛歌择婿"的故事。传说在以前，有位壮族老歌手的闺女长得十分美丽，又很会唱山歌，老人希望挑选一位歌才出众的青年为婿。各地青年歌手纷纷赶来，赛歌求婚，从此就形成了定期的赛歌集会。

Song Fair originated from the singing and dancing activities for worship in clans and tribes times. With the development of society, this primitive ritual group singing and dancing activity transited from "entertaining gods" to "entertaining humans", and transformed from "dancing focus" to "singing focus", which eventually led to the formation of the group-exchanged singing activity. The song fair of Zhuang produced many beautiful stories and tales in its development process, such as "celebrating a bumper harvest year", "son-in-law selecting through singing competition", and "Song Fairy Liu Sanjie passing songs". Among them, the story of "son-in-law selecting through singing competition" is popular, which has told a story of an old Zhuang singer wanted to pick out a son-in-law with outstanding singing ability for his beautiful and singing-talented daughter. Many young boys with singing capability came over to compete and thus formed a regular singing gathering.

가우는 씨족부락시대의 제사성가무활동에서 기원되였다. 사회의 발전과 더불어 원시적인 의식성군체가무는 "유희신"으로부터 "유희인"으로 과도하면서 "무무화"에서 "노래화"로 발전하여 군체성시창가무활동이 형성되였다. 장족가우에는 풍년을 기원하는 기도, 사위를 선택하는 시곡, 가선유삼저 전가 등 장기적인 발전 과정에서 감동적인 전설이 많이 전해져 왔다. 그중 비교적 유행되고 있는 것은 "노래 겨루고 사위 고르기"이야기이다. 전설에 의하면 한 쫭족로가수의 딸이 아주 아름답고 산노래도 잘 불렀는데 로인은 노래재능이 출중한 젊은이를 사위로 고르려 했다고 한다.각지의 청년가수들이 분분히 찾아와 노래시합을 통해 청혼하였는데 이때로부터 정기적인 노래시합 모임이 형성되었다.

歌圩是壮族古老的风俗习惯，凡是较大的壮族聚居区都有歌圩，壮族歌圩主要有以下形式：节日性歌圩，一般在农历正月至五月，秋季的八、九月间的节日里举行；临场性歌圩，在劳动场所、圩市、婚娶之时歌唱；竞赛性歌圩，包括"放球、还球歌圩"、"庙会赛歌"等。有的歌圩则节日性、纪念性、祭祀性兼而有之。其中农历三月三的歌圩最为隆重。

Song Fair is an old custom of Zhuang Ethnic Group and exists in every bigger Zhuang inhabited area. Major forms Zhuang Song Fairs are Festive fairs, which are held in holidays from the first lunar month to the fifth lunar month, and the holidays in August and September, Impromptu song fairs which sung at working places, fairs and wedding, and Competing song fairs which includes "giving and returning ball" song fair and temple singing competition. Some song fairs contains commemorative and sacrificial features, as well as the feature of festival. Among them Song Fair of March the third in lunar month is the grandest.

가우는 좡족의 오래된 풍속습관이다. 비교적 큰 좡족 집단 거주지역에는 모두 거장이 있다. 좡족거장은 주로 다음과 같은 형식이 있다. 축제성 가우는 일반적으로 음력 정월부터 5월, 그리고 가을 8월과 9월 사이의 명절에 거행한다. 림장성가우는 작업장이나 장마당, 혼인과 장가를 갈 때 부르는 노래이다. 경기성가우는 노래장에는 '공놀이ㆍ환구노래장', '묘회시합 노래' 등이 있다. 어떤 노래장은 축일, 기념품, 제사 성격을 모두 갖추고 있다. 그중에서 음력 3월 3일의 노래장이 가장 성대하다.

壮族歌圩的规模有大有小，各地不一，大歌圩有上万人，小歌圩也有数百人。地点有固定的，如圩场、坡地等，也有不固定的，一般选择在离村寨不远的空地、山坡上举行。搭彩棚、摆歌台、抛彩球、择佳偶，别有风情。一次大的歌圩往往延续两三天，白天唱为日歌圩，一般在村外山坡上或田野间举行；晚上唱为夜歌圩，在村中举行。

Song Fairs of Zhuang vary in size, place and number of participants. Bigger Song Fairs may attract ten thousands of people, while smaller one may just have hundreds of people involved. In terms of holding places, fair sites, slopes are the fixed ones, while a clearing near the village and a slope of the hill are also the choice. It is different and interesting to put up a shed, arrange a singing stage, throw color balls and pursue a mate. A big Song fair often lasts for two days, during which day time singing is usually held in the slopes out of the village or in the fields, while night time singing takes place in the village.

가우는 쫭족의 오래된 풍속습관이다. 비교적 큰 쫭족 집단 거주지역에는 모두 거장이 있다. 쫭족거장은 주로 다음과 같은 형식이 있다. 축제성

가우는 일반적으로 음력 정월부터 5월, 그리고 가을 8월과 9월 사이의 명절에 거행 한다. 림장성 가우는 작업 장이나 장마당, 혼인과 장가를 갈 때 부르는 노래이다. 경기성 가우는 노래장에는 '공놀이 · 환 구 노 래 장', '묘회시합노래' 등이 있다. 어떤 노래장은 축일, 기념품, 제사 성격을 모두 갖추고 있다. 그중에서 음력 3월 3일의 노래장이 가장 성대하다.

壮族歌圩活动的内容主要有三方面，一是歌场交情，即倚歌择配。二是赛歌赏歌，有盘歌、猜歌、对子歌、连故事和别具特色的抢歌、斗歌等。三是文体自娱歌圩，圩期伴有抛绣球、抢花炮、斗蛋、博扇活动等，甚至还有壮剧、师公戏、采茶戏等文艺演出。

There are three major topics in Song Fairs of Zhuang. The first one is emotion exchange through singing, which can also be called mating through singing; the second one is singing competition and singing appreciation, which include Pange, song guessing, song pairing, story making by singing and the distinctive song racing and contesting; the third one is Song Fair for entertaining, such as throwing color silk balls, grabbing firecrackers, playing eggs and exchanging fans, together with art performances of Zhuang opera, Shigong opera and Tea-picking opera.

Note: Pange: an old antiphonal style of singing used by young girls and boys to express their passion and love to each other in Miao Ethnic Group.

광족가우활동에는 주로 세가지 내용이 포함된다. 하나는 노래장에서의 친분, 즉 노래에 따라 배우자를 선택하는 행위이다. 둘째는 싸이가요 (싸이가요)로 반가, 답가, 대자가(對子歌), 연고사와 특색 있는 빼앗기 노래, 투가 등이 있다. 셋째는 문체자오락 노래장인데 장날에 동반된다. 수놓은 공 던지기, 화포 빼앗기, 투단, 박선 행사 등은 물론 쟝극 · 사공희 · 채차희 등의 문예 공연까지 있다.

歌圩是壮族民歌的自然载体, 它已成为壮族的传统文化娱乐活动的代表形式, 造就了壮族特有的"歌圩文化", 对于壮族各类传统民歌的产生、传承与发展具有重要的作用。同时它又是壮族民间文学的宝库, 对了解和研究壮族古代社会生活具有重要的价值。歌圩还为广大民众特别是青年提供了学习山歌和展示歌才的场所, 满足了他们崇尚山歌、诗性思维的心理需求。

Song Fair of Zhuang is the natural carrier of Zhuang folk songs, and a representative form of traditional Zhuang entertaining activity, from which a unique Zhuang style song fair culture is made. It plays a significant role in the creation, inheritance and development of various folk songs of Zhuang Ethnic Group. On one hand, it is a Zhuang folk literature treasure, which provides important value for understanding and studying the ancient social life of Zhuang people. On the other hand, it not only provides places for Zhuang youth to learn folk songs and present their singing, but also meets their psychological needs of respecting folk songs and poetry.

가우는 쫭족 민요의 자연 매개체로서 쫭족의 전통문화 오락 활동의 대표 형식이 되었고 쫭족 특유의 "거우문화"를 탄생시켰으며 쫭족의 각종 전통 민요의 발생, 전승과 발전에 중요한 역할을 하고 있다. 또한 광족민간 문학의 보물고로서 광족의 고대사회생활을 요해하고 연구하는데 중요한 가치가 있다. 노래장은 또한 광범한 민중, 특히 청년들에게 산요를 배우고 노래 재능을 전시할 수 있는 장소를 제공하여 그들이 산요와 시적 사유를 숭상하는 심리적 요구를 만족시켜 준다.

22. 壮族蚂拐节

Maguai Festival of Zhuang Ethnic Group
[入选时间: 2006　Time: 2006
遗产名录: 第一批国家级非物质文化遗产名录
Heritage Category: List of the first batch of National Intangible Cultural Heritage.
地域:　河池　　Region:　Hechi]

壮族蚂拐节，又叫蛙婆节或青蛙节，主要流行于广西西北部红水河流域沿岸一带的壮族聚居区，是壮族先民青蛙崇拜的遗俗。人们通过祭拜青蛙，祈求风调雨顺、五谷丰登、人畜兴旺。

The Maguai Festival of Zhuang Ethnic Group, also known as Wapo Festival or Frog Festival, is mainly popular in the Zhuang-inhabited areas along the Hongshui River Basin in Northwest Guangxi. It is an old custom of worshiping frogs handed down by the Zhuang ancestors. People worship frogs to pray for fine weather, bumper grain harvest and flourishing population and livestock.

장족 마괴절, 개구리아줌마절 또는 개구리절이라고도 하는데 주로 유행 광서 서북부 홍수 하류 역 연안 일대 쫭 족 집 거구는 장족 선민 개구리 숭배의 유풍이 존재한다. 사람들은 개구리에게 제를 지내면서 날씨가 좋고, 오곡이 풍성하며, 사람과 가축의 흥성을 기원했다.

壮族传说认为掌管风雨的是青蛙女神，并把青蛙称为蚂拐，认为蚂拐是雷王的女儿，掌管雨水，使大地风调雨顺。相传，神祖布洛陀的大儿子在敢壮山的西部开辟了一块田地，田地在秋收的时节，庄稼都被蝗虫给吃了。布洛陀的大儿子跑去请教布洛陀该怎么办。布洛陀叫天山的雷王派遣青蛙（蚂拐）下凡守护田间地头，害虫来了他就吃掉害虫。如遇到干旱它就叫，呼唤天上下雨，后来这只青蛙被蛇咬死了，布洛陀就把青蛙的遗体装在盒子里，放进轿子里绕着村庄行走，足足走了一个月以示纪念。布洛陀告诫人们要依照传统纪念青蛙，这就是蚂拐节的由来。

Zhuang people call frog "Maguai" in their language. According to Zhuang legend, the Frog Goddess, the daughter of God of Thunder, was in charge of the wind and rain, to maintain the earth in good weather. It was said that the eldest son of Buluotuo opened up a field in the west of Ganzhuang Mountain. When the autumn harvest came, the crops were eaten by locusts. Buluotuo's eldest son went to ask him for help. He asked Thunder God to send a frog to guard the fields and eat the insects. If there was a drought, the frog would cry and call for rain. Later, the frog was bitten to death by a snake. Buluotuo put the frog body in a box. To remember it, Buluotuo ask people to carry it around the village in a sedan chair for a month. Buluotuo told people to memorize frogs according to this customs, which has become a tradition to offer sacrifices to Maguai by celebrating Maguai Festive every year.

장족 전설은 장족전설에서는 비바람을 관장하는 여신은 개구리여신이라고 한다. 개구리를 蚂拐라고, 뇌왕의 딸로, 비를 다스려, 대지에 좋은 날씨를 이루었도다. 전하는데 의하면 포락타의 큰아들이 용장산서부에 밭떼기를 일구었는데 추수철이 되면 메뚜기들에게 농작물을 먹였다고 한다. 포락타에게 어떻게 해야 할지 물었다. 개구리 브 타 천 산 이란 뇌왕 파견 내려 밭머리를 지키 해충 왔으니 그 먹다.나중에 개구리가 뱀에 물려 죽자 포락타는 개구리의 시체를 상자에 넣고 가마에 넣어 한 달 동안 기념으로 마을을 돌아다녔다. 브 타들을 전통에 따라 기념 개구리, 이것이 바로 蚂 절의 유래.

蚂拐节一般从大年初一起，至二月初二结束，节日期间，人们穿上节日盛装，以祭青蛙为主要活动，敲锣打鼓，召集四方歌友，欢聚一堂，歌声遍野。蚂拐节主要环节大体分为找蚂拐、祭蚂拐、游拜蚂拐、丧蚂拐和篝火铜鼓山歌会等一系列的蚂拐崇拜活动，活动期间还兼有唱山歌、碰彩蛋、打陀螺、民俗表演、民间游戏、敲击铜鼓的民俗活动。有的地区还出现戴着青蛙面具的男女青蛙神、青蛙将军及其他神灵，分别跳着各种舞蹈。

Maguai Festival usually starts at the beginning of the Lunar New Year and ends on the second day of the second month in lunar calendar. During the festival, the main activity is sacrificing frogs, and people dress up in costumes to beat gongs and drums and sing with friends from all over the country. Everyone enjoys this joyous gathering and their sounds of singing can be heard everywhere. The main part of this festival includes a series of worshiping activities for frogs such as looking for the frogs, sacrificing the frogs, parading the frogs, burying the frogs and folk songs fair with bronze drum bonfire. There are some other folk activities like singing the folk songs, bumping the colored eggs, playing spinning top, folklore performances, folk games and taping on a bronze drum. In some areas, there are also activities in which people wearing frog masks, dressing up and dancing respectively as frog gods and goodness, frog general as well as other gods.

마꽈이절 일반 대 초 함께 2월 초 중 2학년까지, 명절 기간에는 사람들이 명절 성장을 입고 제사 개구리를 주요 활동으로, 북을 치고 꽹과리를 울리며 사방으로 소집, 즐겁게 한자리에 모여 노래들 전체다. 잠자리 마꽈이절 주요 고리에 크게 찾 마꽈이, 제사 마꽈이, 수영 배마꽈이·장례 마꽈이절과 화톳불 가 민요 등 일련의 마꽈이 숭배 활동, 활동 기간도 겸하 민요를 부딪쳐 달걀, 팽이를 치다, 민속 공연, 민간 게임, 가 두드리는 민속놀이다. 개구리 가면을 쓴 남녀 청개구리 신과 청개구리 장군, 그리고 다른 신들이 나타나 각기 춤을 추기도 한다.

每当农历正月初一黎明,人们就敲着铜鼓成群结队去田里找冬眠的青蛙。据说,先找到青蛙的人是幸运的,被誉为雷王的女婿"蚂拐郎",成为该年蚂拐的首领。首领要带着大家点燃烟炮,以向雷王报告人间祭蚂拐的喜讯。人们把这只青蛙接回村,放入花轿中。由初一到正月底,白天孩子们抬着青蛙游村,向每家每户贺喜;晚上,则抬到蚂拐亭下,人们跳蚂拐舞和唱蚂拐歌,以示为蚂拐守灵。守灵、游村的活动进行到第25天后,蚂拐节便进入高潮。这天,人们选择吉时,抬着花轿到青蛙下葬的地方,打开去年葬蛙的宝棺,如果青蛙的骨头呈金黄色,便预示今年是好年景,全场顿时铜鼓齐名,同声欢呼。如果蛙骨呈灰色或黑色,便表示年景不好,于是人们就烧香祈求消灾降福。接着举行新青蛙的的下葬仪式。葬礼之后,男女老少一起围着篝火唱歌跳舞,送蚂拐的灵魂上天。

Every dawn of the first day of the first lunar month, people look for the hibernated frogs in groups, tapping the bronze drums. It is said that the one who find the frog is lucky and he will be regarded as the son-in-law of the God of Thunder and

"The Boy of Frog" (Maguailang), becoming the leader of frogs of the year. He will lead people to light the fireworks and firecrackers to tell this good news to the Lord of Thunder. People invite this frog to their village and put it into a bridal sedan chair. Children carry the sedan chair to every family for congratulation in the daytime. At night, the sedan chair is carried to the frog pavilion, where people perform frog dance and sing frog songs to keep vigil beside the coffin for the frog. The festival reaches its climax until the 25th days of the festival, on which people choose the auspicious moment and carry the sedan chair to the burial place. When the frog's coffin of last year was open, if the bones left is golden, it means they will come to a harvest year, while if it is gray or black, it will predict to be a bad year. Then, people will burn incense to pray for the dispel of disasters and arrival of blessings. Next, a new frog's funeral will be held and after that, people will sing and dance around the bonfire to send the soul of the frog to heaven.

음력 정월 초하룻날이 밝으면 사람들은 동고를 치며 겨울잠을 자는 개구리를 찾아 떼를 지어 논으로 나갔다. 이 먼저 개구리를 찾는 것은 다행스러운, 뇌왕으로 불리는 사위 '蚂拐'화랑, 이 蚂拐의 두목으로 되였다. 두목이 모두를 데리고 담배에 불을 포에게 뇌왕 잠자리 인간 제물 蚂拐 희소식을 보고할 예정이다. 사람들은 이 개구리를 마을로 데려와 꽃가마에 태웠다. 초하루부터 정월 말까지는 낮에는 아이들이 개구리를 들고 마을을 돌아다니며 집집마다 축하해 주었다. 밤은 잠자리에 들 蚂拐 정자 밑 잠자리들이 뛰 蚂拐 춤과 노래를 蚂拐 노래, 잠자리로 표시의 넋을 기리다. 빈소, 헤엄을 촌까지 활동할 제25일 후 蚂拐절을 고조시켰다. 청개구리의 뼈가 황금색을 띠면 올해 작황이 좋음을 예시한다. 장내를 가득 메우고 일제히 환호한다. 만약 개구리뼈가 회색이나 검은색을 띠면 연수가 좋지 않음을 뜻하므로 사람들은 향을 피워 재화를 없애고 복을 내리기를 빈다. 이어 새 개구리의 하관 의식이 거행되었다. 장례식 이후 모닥불 주위에서 남녀노소가 함께 노래하고 춤추며 잠자리를 蚂拐의 영혼이 하늘로 올라간다.

23. 壮族铜鼓习俗

The bronze drum custom of the Zhuang Ethnic Group
[入选时间: 2006 Time: 2006
遗产名录: 第一批国家级非物质文化遗产名录
Heritage Category: List of the first batch of National Intangible Cultural Heritage.
地域: 河池 Region: Hechi]

壮族铜鼓习俗是壮族民众敲击使用铜鼓、收藏铜鼓、铸造铜鼓等一系列与铜鼓崇拜信仰有关的民俗行为。铜鼓是中国南方少数民族打击式乐器中的一种，集重器、神器、乐器、礼器等多种文化功能于一身。其历史悠久，源远流长，创始期约在春秋时代，最初的形态来源于炊具铜釜。当代壮族铜鼓习俗的分布以红水河流域为核心，集中分布在广西河池市东兰县、天峨县、南丹县、巴马县、凤山县、大化县和广西百色市田林县、隆林县、西林县等壮族聚居地区。

The bronze drum custom of the Zhuang Ethnic Group is a series of folk behaviors related to the worship of bronze drum, such as the play, the collection, and the casting of bronze drum. The bronze drum is one of the percussion instruments of the ethnic minorities in southern China. It is a combination of various cultural functions, such as the cultural function of the Heavy Instruments, Sacred Instruments, Musical Instruments and Sacrificial Vessels. The bronze drum has a long history. It was founded around the Spring and Autumn Period, and its original form came from the copper kettle of cooking utensils. The distribution of contemporary Zhuang bronze drum customs is centered around the Hongshui River basin, which is popular in the Zhuang Ethnic Group's gathering areas in Guangxi such as Donglan County, Tiane County, Nandan County, Bama County, Fengshan County, Dahua County in Hechi city and Tianlin County, Longlin County, Xilin County in Baise city.

좡족 동고 풍습은 좡족 민중들이 동고를 치고 사용하거나, 수집하고, 주조하는 등 동고 숭배와 신앙과 관련된 일련의 민속 행위이다. 동고는 중국 남방 소수민족의 타식악기 중 하나로 중기, 신기, 악기, 예기 등 다양한 문화적 기능이 집약돼 있다. 유구한 역사를 갖고 있는 바 그 창기는 대략 춘추시대이며 최초의 형태는 취사도구인 구리솥에서 기원되었다. 당대 좡족 동고 풍속의 분포는 홍수하 유역을 중심으로 광시 허츠시 동란현, 천아현, 남단현, 바마현, 펑산현, 대화현과 광시 바이써시 톈린현, 룽린현, 서린현 등 좡족 집거 지역에 집중적으로 분포되어 있다.

壮族民众敲击使用铜鼓的习俗主要发生在春节、三月三歌圩节、蚂拐节、七月十四、八月十五等重大传统节日和进新房、新婚、祭祖、庆典、重大迎宾活动、工程开工竣工等仪式中。其内容十分丰富，有铸造习俗、使用习俗、歌舞习俗、传承习俗等多种类型；具有很强的艺术价值，包括造型艺术、音乐艺术、舞蹈艺术、神话传说等艺术内容；主要以建筑活动、婚恋嫁娶、丧葬祭祖、节日庆典等具体文化时空为载体；具有娱神、镇邪、娱人、礼人和象征权力地位、财富等民俗功能。

The custom of playing bronze drums by the Zhuang people mainly occurs during the Spring Festival, Double Three Festival, Maguai Festival, July 14th(lunar), August 15th(lunar) and other major traditional festivals. It also played in new house moving, weddings, ancestor worships, celebrations, grand welcome activities, commencement and completion of the project, and other ceremonies. It has rich contents, including casting customs, playing customs, singing and dancing customs, inheriting customs and other types. It also has strong artistic value in building, music, dance, myths and legends. It is mainly based on the specific cultural space-time such as architectural activities, marriage, funeral and ancestor worship, festival celebrations and so on. It has the folk functions of entertaining gods, dispelling evil spirits, entertaining people, ritualizing people and symbolizing power status and wealth.

쫭족 민중봉기가 사용 두드리는 풍습에 주로 발생설, 3월 노래장절, 蚂拐절, 7월 14일, 8월 15일 등 중대한 전통 명절 제사와 새집에 신혼, 축제, 중대한 영빈 활동, 공사 착공 준공 등 식에서다. 그 내용은 매우 풍부한데, 주조 풍속, 사용 풍속, 가무 풍속, 전승 풍속 등 여러 가지 유형이 있다. 조형예술, 음악예술, 무용예술, 신화전설 등 예술내용을 포함하여 아주 강한 예술적 가치가 있다. 주로 건축 활동, 결혼, 결혼, 장례, 조상제사, 명절 축제 등 구체적인 문화 시간과 공간을 담체로 한다. 신(神)을 즐겁게 하고, 악을 진하게 하고, 사람을 즐겁게 하고, 예인을 하고, 권력과 지위, 재부를 상징하는 등 민속적인 기능을 가지고 있다.

红水河沿岸的壮家, 几乎村村有铜鼓, 据资料统计, 2015年全世界馆藏传世铜鼓2400多面, 其中我国馆藏量1400面, 广西馆藏量900多面。铜鼓是壮族人民心中的神物。铜鼓文化是壮族的"活文化", 从不同的侧面反映了壮族的经济状况和文化面貌, 体现了壮族独特的创造力。铜鼓文化流传时间之长、范围之广、影响之深, 世所罕见。

Almost every village in Zhuang's family along the Hongshui River has bronze drums. According to statistics, more than 2400 bronze drums which are handed down from ancient times are collected in the museums around the world in 2015, among which 1400 are found in China with 900 in Guangxi. The bronze drum is a sacred object in the heart of Zhuang people. Bronze drum culture is living culture of Zhuang, reflecting the economy and culture of Zhuang Ethnic Group. It is rare in the world for its long circulation, wide range and far-reaching influence.

홍수하연안의 쫭자에는 마을마다 동고가 있다. 통계에 따르면 2015년 전 세계 소장된 동고는 2,400여면이며 그중 중국의 소장량은 1,400여면이고 광서의 소장량은 900여면이다. 동고는 쫭족 국민들 마음속의 신물이다. 동고문화는 쫭족의 살아 있는 문화로 다양한 측면에서 쫭족의 경제 상황과 문화 면모를 반영하고 있으며, 쫭족의 독특한 창조력을 나타내고 있다. 동고문화가 유전된 시간의 길이와 범위의 넓이, 영향력의 깊이는 세계에서 보기 드물다.

24. 宾阳炮龙节

Firecracker Dragon Festival in Binyang
[入选时间: 2008　Time: 2008
遗产名录: 第二批国家级非物质文化遗产名录
Heritage Category: List of the Second batch of National Intangible Cultural Heritage.
地域: 宾阳　Region: Binyang]

宾阳炮龙节是广西宾阳县独有的一个传统节日，是汉族、壮族文化融合共生的综合性民间节庆，于每年农历正月十一举行。

Firecracker Dragon Festival in Binyang, a special traditional festival in Binyang County Guangxi, falls on the 11th day of the first month of the lunar New Year, which is an original local festival celebrated by both the Han and Zhuang ethnic groups.

빈양포룡제는 광시 빈양현만의 전통명절로서 한족과 쫭족 문화가 융합되고 공존하는 종합적인 민간축제로 음력 11월에 거행된다.

宾阳炮龙节历史悠久，起源说法不一，但流传较广，被大家较为认同的说法是起源于宋朝狄青与侬智高昆仑关大战。宋皇佑五年（公元1053年）宋朝名将狄青为了麻痹"据关造反"的壮族首领侬智高，时值元宵前夕，下令大办酒席宴客三天，并令士兵扎龙起舞，号召百姓家家户户鞭炮齐鸣、助庆狂欢，宾州城内一派欢腾景象。当夜二鼓，狄青率领精兵突袭昆仑关，三鼓时分夺下昆仑关。宾州城居民从此认为舞炮龙吉祥，每年此时必舞炮龙以求喜庆，狂欢不断，流传至今。

The Festival has a long history and many stories are told about its origin. One popular and well accepted story is from the battle of the Kunlun Pass between Di Qing and Nong Zhigao in Song Dynasty. In the 5th year of Huangyou Period of Song Dynasty (1053 A.D.), Di Qing, a famous general of Song, ordered to hold feasts for three days and commanded the soldiers to make dragons for dancing, in order to slacken the vigilance of Nong Zhigao, the leader of Zhuang who occupied the pass and rebelled. He also asked all the families to set off firecrackers and created a carnival scene on Lantern Festival Eve. After nine o' clock that night, Di Qing led the elite troops to raid Kunlun Pass and at eleven o' clock he took over Kunlun Pass. Since then, people in Binzhou believed that performing firecracker dragon dance is fortunate. Thus people would do so for festivity every year and the tradition has been passed down until now.

빈양포룡절은 역사가 유구하고 기원설은 다양하지만 널리 전해지고 있다. 사람들이 비교적 인정하는 설은 송나라 적청(狄青)과 농지고(농지고) 곤륜관(昆崙관)의 큰 싸움이다. 송나라 황우 5년(1053년), 송나라 명장 디칭(디 청)은'관내에 주둔해 반란을 일으킨 '좡족 수령 눙즈가오(농)를 마비시키기 위해 정월 대보름 전날 밤, 3일 동안 큰 연회를 베풀도록 명령했다. 병사들은 자룡에게 춤을 추게 하고, 백성들은 집집마다 폭죽을 터뜨려 즐겁게 놀도록 했다. 그날 밤 2고 때에 적청은 정병을 거느리고 곤륜관을 기습하여 3고 때에 곤륜관을 탈취하였다. 펜실베니아 주민들은 이때로부터 룡폭죽을 춤추면 상서롭다고 여겨 매년 룡폭죽을 춤추며 경사를 경축하는데 이는 오늘날까지 계속되고 있다.

宾阳炮龙节的主要习俗表演活动有游彩架、灯会、舞炮龙等。舞炮龙由总指挥（亦称会首）发号施令，舞龙者均赤膊上阵，头戴如清朝官兵之帽（均为竹编并涂抹黑色）。炮龙以龙珠、龙牌、锣鼓、文武场开路，照明及护龙队首尾随龙而进，炮龙所到之处，各家各户夹道相迎，将事先准备好的鞭炮拿出来燃放，抛向炮龙，有"炮声不停，龙舞不止"之说，故称炮龙。炮龙定于当晚七时在庙宇或社稷之处开光，由会首（或师人）咬破公鸡之冠，以鸡冠之血点亮开光龙眼后，方可万炮齐鸣，龙亦方可腾跃而起。

The major customs and performances of Binyang Firecracker Dragon Festival include parading color frame, visiting lantern fair, and performing firecracker dragon dance. Firecracker dragon dance is led and commanded by a chief (also known as the head of a folk organization), and all the performers are bare-chested, wearing hats which like the officers and soldiers' hats of Qing dynasty (actually made of bamboo and painted black). The firecracker dragon is started with the dragon ball, dragon plate, gongs and drums, WenWu Chang, and the lighting and guarding team follows at the head and end of the dragon. While the dragon dance going on, local residents line the streets to welcome and they set off the firecrackers prepared in advance, throwing to the dragon. It is said that the dragon dance won't stop until the firecracker ends, so it earns the name of firecracker dragon. At seven o 'clock in the evening, the firecracker dragon is scheduled to be consecrated by the chief (or master) in the temple or the place of the god of the earth and grain. The chief bites the rooster's crown, and use the blood to consecrate the dragon's eye. Only after that, thousands of firecrackers can be fired together, and the dragon dance can be started.

Note: Wenwu Chang are two divisions of the orchestra in traditional Chinese operas: Wen Chang is civil division consisting of stringed and wind instruments, while Wu Chang is military division consisting of percussion instruments.

빈양 용발포 축제의 주요 풍속 공연 활동에는 채색 받침놀이 · 등불 놀이 · 용발포 춤 등이 있다. 룡포를 추는 무용은 총지휘(회수라고도 함.) 가 호령을 내리는데 모두 웃통을 벗고 머리에는 청나라 장병들의 모자(모두 대나무로 엮고 검은색으로 칠하였음.)를 썼다. 포룡(砲龍)은 룡주 · 룡패 · 징 · 북 · 문무장으로 길을 열고 조명과 호룡(호위대)을 시작으로 용을 따라 들어간다. 포룡이 도착하는 곳이면 집집마다 연도에 늘어서서 마중을 하며 미리 준비한 폭죽을 꺼내 터뜨리고 포룡에 던지는데, '포성이 멈추지 않고 룡이 춤을 춘다'는 말이 있어 '포룡'이라고 한다. 포 용 (砲)은 그날 저녁 7시에 사당이나 사직에서 빛을 발하게 하는데, 회의 (또는 스승) 가 수탉의 관을 물어서 찢고, 볏의 혈점으로 용의 눈을 밝히면, 비로소 만포가 일제히 울리고, 용이 도약하여 솟아오른다.

宾阳炮龙节有东方"狂欢节"之称，堪称中华一绝。如今，炮龙节的影响力逐步扩大，活动内容日益多样化，千年"炮龙"在传承保护的同时也正带来更多民俗热潮，师公剧、八音文武场、采茶戏、踩高跷、对山歌等极具宾阳特色的民间文艺先后融入节庆之中，有力地推动了当地民俗文化的发展。

Firecracker Dragon Festival in Binyang is known as the "Carnival" of the East and is a unique event in China. Nowadays, it has gradually gained its influence and as the contents of the activity becomes increasingly diversified, the conservation and inheritance of the thousand-year old "firecracker dragon" have brought in more and more folk customs with strong feature of Binyang County, such as the Master's Opera, Bayin Wen Wu Chang, Tea Picking Opera, Stilts Walking, Singing Folk Songs, which has effectively promoted the development of local folk culture.

방의 '카니발'로 불리는 빈양 포룡제는 중화 일품이다. 현재, 포룡제의 영향력은 점차적으로 확대되고, 행사 내용은 나날이 다양해지고 있다. 천년의 "포룡"은 전승과 보호를 동시에 더 많은 민속 붐을 가져오고 있다. 사공극(师公劇), 팔음문무장(八音文武場), 채차희(彩茶戏), 높은 나무다리 밟기, 산간 노래 등 빈양의 특색이 강한 민간문예가 선후로 축제 속에 녹아 들어 현지 민속문화의 발전을 강력하게 추진했다.

25. 龙胜瑶族服饰

Costumes of Longsheng Yao Ethnic Group
[入选时间：2014　Time: 2014
遗产名录：第四批国家级非物质文化遗产扩展项目名录
Heritage Category: Extended list of the fourth batch of National Intangible Cultural Heritage.
地域：桂林　　Region：Guilin]

龙胜瑶族服饰制作技艺特指红瑶服饰制作技艺，流传在广西桂林市龙胜各族自治县的和平乡、马堤乡、泗水乡、江底乡等瑶族村寨，当地的瑶族自称"忧"，因妇女身穿红色锦衣花裙俗称红瑶。

Longsheng Yao costume making technique refers to Red Yao costume making technique, which is popular among Yao villages in townships of Heping, Madi, Sishui, Jiangdi in Longsheng Autonomous County of Guilin, Guangxi. The local Yao people call themselves "You", and they are commonly known as Red Yao, because Yao women are fond of wearing red embroidered dresses.

룡승요족 복식제작기법은 특히 홍요의 복식제작기예를 가리키는데 광시성 계림시 룡승각족 자치현의 허핑향, 마디향, 쓰수이향, 장디향 등의 요족 마을에 널리 전해졌으며 현지의 요족은 스스로를 '우'라고 불렀으며 여성들이 붉은 금의화 치마를 입고 있기 때문에 홍요라고 속칭한다.

红瑶服饰有鲜明的穿着特点，其服饰有男女之分，男人以素色为主，最常见的是青衣和青裤。妇女喜好五色，花色斑斓多彩。服饰特色集中体现在妇女的衣着上，妇女上杉下裙，上衣多花，上衣有饰衫、花衣、青衣和双衣四种。上衣纹饰繁复，富有想象力，工艺别具一格，既不需要描图打稿，也不需要模具，全凭一双慧眼，一双巧手。

Red Yao's costumes have their unique characteristics, which are different by gender. Yao men tend to wear plain costumes, among which the most common ones are blue tops and blue trousers, whereas women prefer costumes that are diverse in both color and pattern. Consequently, Yao women's clothing basically carries the features of Yao costumes. Yao women usually wear Chinese jacket with skirt, and their jackets could be divided into four types, including brocaded jackets, embroidered jackets, plain jackets, and interlining jackets. Made by unique techniques, Yao jackets are quite complicated and imaginative in decoration patterns. Without a draft or a template, they are totally made by Yao people with their discerning eyes and skillful hands.

홍요의 옷차림은 선명한 옷차림특징을 갖고 있는 바 남녀의 구분이 있으며 남자는 흰색을 위주로하고 청의와 청바지를 가장 흔히 볼 수 있다. 여자들은 오색을 좋아한다. 복식 특색은 여성의 복장에서 집중적으로 구현되는데, 여성의 옷에는 삼나무 위에 치마가 있고, 저고리는 꽃이 많으며, 저고리는 장삼 (장식), 화의 (花衣), 청의와 쌍의 (双衣) 네 종류가 있다. 저고리는 무늬장식이 복잡하고 상상력이 풍부하며 공예가 남다른 풍격을 갖고 있어 그림을 그릴 필요도 없고 주형을 만들 필요도 없이 모두 혜안과 솜씨에 의거하였다.

红瑶服饰制作的主要传统技艺有纺织、蜡染、刺绣三种，均为手工。纺织是纺纱织布、织锦的技艺，织布以白棉线为材料织布作为花衣、素衣的原料,织锦以蚕丝线为材料白线作经、红线作纬、花线织图织成锦布作为锦衣的原料。蜡染以沸蜡在白布点绘出各种花纹图案,而后将绘制好的布投入蓝靛缸中浸染,待布受蓝后取出洗净晒干,再用碱水浸泡去蜡,即做成花裙所需要的斑花布。

There are three main traditional making techniques of Red Yao costumes, namely, textile, batik and embroidery, all of which are handmade. Textile manufacturing refers to the technique of weaving and brocading. Cloth white cotton thread is weaved as the material of embroidered clothes and plain clothes; white silk thread is brocaded as warp, red silk thread as weft and multicolored silk thread as patterns, which makes the material of brocade clothes.Batik is a wax-resist dyeing technique in which hot and liquid wax is used to draw various patterns on white cloth, and then the cloth is put in a indigo vat for dip dyeing. The cloth won't be washed and dried until it turns blue. Finally, the cloth is soaked in alkaline water to remove wax, thus the spotted cloth is obtained for embroidered skirt making.

홍요복식제작의 주요 전통기법은 방직, 랍염, 자수 세 가지인데 모두 수공이다. 방직은 실을 뽑아 천을 짜거나 비단을 짜는 기술로서, 비단을 짤 때는 흰면실을 재료로 하여 천을 짜서 꽃옷·소복의 원료로 하고, 비단을 짤 때는 누에실을 재료로 하여 흰실 날실을 만들고, 붉은실 날실을 만들며, 꽃실 날실을 짜서 비단을 만들어 비단의 날옷의 원료로 한다. 랍염 백포에 랍을 끓여 여러가지 꽃무늬도안을 그린다. 그어진 천을 남색염료항아리에 넣어 염색을 한후 빨아 말린 후 염소화수에 담가서 얼룩무늬천을 만든다.

刺绣瑶族妇女称之为挑花，用于制作花衣，以蓝布为底，用各色蚕丝线挑绣图案，绣时无需画图，依底布的纱路经纬线确定图案位置，然后用各色丝线绣出绚丽多姿的图案。反绣为刺绣技法，绣时在背面运针，正面成图案，以平整、细密、生动为优。因图案集中在肩部，以方框框住形如坎肩，腰背两侧各绣有如拳大的方印（虎爪印），故名为花衣。衣、裙、头巾、包肚、腰带、围裙、围裙带、东摆、裙摆、脚绑、脚绑带、花鞋等整套的龙胜瑶族服饰，均用纺织、蜡染、刺绣的手工技艺制作。

Embroidery, which is called cross-stitch by Yao women, is a technique used in making embroidered clothes. Silk threads of various colors are used to stitch splendid patterns on a piece of blue cloth, which is considered as the base. No draft is made for embroidering with the position of the patterns determined by the warp and weft yarn of the base cloth and brilliant colored patterns are made. Another embroidery technique used by Yao people is cross-stitch on the back, in which needles are carried on the back and patterns are formed on the front. A pattern that is smooth, fine and vivid is considered as a premium embroidery. Since the patterns majorly fall on the shoulder part shaped like a vest with a square frame, and both sides of the waist and the back parts are stitched by the patterns of the fist-sized tiger claws in square form, the garment receives its name "embroidered clothes". The whole set of Longsheng Yao costumes, including the upper clothes, skirts, headscarves, belly wraps, belts, aprons, apron straps, hemlines, foot ties, foot straps, embroidered shoes, and so on, are all made with manual techniques of weaving and spinning, batik and embroidery.

자수 요족녀성들을 십자수라고 하는데 꽃옷을 만드는데 남색천을 밑받침으로 여러 가지 색깔의 명주실로 도안을 수 놓는데 그림을 그릴 필요가 없고 천의 실길을 따라 위도선을 따라 도안의 위치를 확정한 후, 여러 가지 색깔의 명주실로 화려하고 다채로운 도안을 수놓는다. 역수는 자수 기법으로, 수를 놓을 때 뒤면에서 바늘을 옮기고 정면에서 도안을 만들며, 평평하고 세밀하며 생동감이 있어야 한다. 도안이 어깨부위에 집중되어 있고 조끼모양처럼 네모난 테두리로 둘려져 있으며 허리등 량쪽에는 주먹만한 크기의 네모난 무늬(호랑이발자국)가 수놓아져 있어 화의라고 부른다. 옷, 치마, 두건, 배주머니, 허리띠, 앞치마, 앞치마띠, 동자락, 치마자락, 발묶음, 발본대, 꽃신 등 룡승요족 복식은 모두 방직, 랍염, 자수 등의 수공 기술로 제작된다.

26. 钦州跳岭头

Tiao Lingtou in Qinzhou

[入选时间：2014　Time: 2014

遗产名录：第四批国家级非物质文化遗产扩展项目名录

Heritage Category: Extended list of the fourth batch of National Intangible Cultural Heritage.

地域：钦州　Region: Qinzhou]

跳岭头是钦州市一带汉族、壮族文化融合共生的综合性民族民间节庆习俗活动，以豆鼓为主要打击乐器，主要流传于桂西南壮、汉族杂居的钦州、灵山、浦北等地。跳岭头是傩文化的活化石，沿袭了商代傩舞的基本特征，是桂西南地区独特的民间表演艺术。

Tiao Lingtou (Dancing at the Hillside) is a folk activity in Qinzhou, Guangxi Zhuang Autonomous Region, where the Han and Zhuang cultures merge and coexist. With Dou Drum as its main percussion instrument, it is mainly popular in Qinzhou, Lingshan, Pubei and other places in the southwest Guangxi where Zhuang and Han people co-inhabited. Tiao Lingtou is a living fossil of Nuo culture, carrying the basic characteristics of Nuo dance in the Shang Dynasty, making it a unique folk performing art in southwest Guangxi.

The Dou drum is a kind of pottery drum similar in shape to the "dou", a sacrificial vessel in the Neolithic Age.

점링터우는 친저우시 일대의 한족, 좡족 문화가 융합되어 공존하는 종합적인 민족 민간 축제 풍속 활동이다. 콩고(頭鼓)를 주요 타악기로 하며 주로 구이저우 서남부 좡족과 한족이 잡거하는 친저우, 링산, 푸베이 등지에서 널리 전해졌다. 도령두는 나무문화의 살아있는 화석으로서 상조시기 나무의 기본 특징을 답습한 것으로서 광서서남지역의 독특한 민간공연예술이다.

"岭头"即村边山坡，是跳傩舞的地方。古时，跳岭头多在八月中秋节这天进行，所以八月十五也叫做"岭头节"。如今，活动时间已经改变，从八月初二到十月二十日，每年持续两个多月，是一年中时间跨度最大的节日，各村屯过节的日期不一，但内容相似。举办"跳岭头"的村子，家家户户杀猪宰牛，大宴宾客。民间认为谁家邀请到的宾客最多，谁家当年就最有运气，因此除了全村人参加外，邻村和外地的汉族、壮族群众也赶来参加。

"Lingtou" as the hillside in the village, is the place for Nuo dance. In ancient times, It was usually performed on the Mid-Autumn Festival in August, so August 15 was also called "Lingtou Festival". Now, the time of the activity has changed, from the second day of August to the 20th of October, which lasts for more than two months every year. It is the festival with the largest span of time in a year. The dates of festivals vary in different villages, whereas the contents are similar. In the village where "Tiao Lingtou" is performed, every household would feast guests by killing pigs and cows for food. People believe that the more guests they could invite the luckier they would be in that year, and besides people in the same village, the Han and Zhuang villagers from the neighboring villages and other places also came to attend.

'靈头'는 마을 옆의 산비탈로 나무를 추는 곳이다. 옛날에는 넘기를 팔월

중추절에 많이 해서 팔월 보름날을 '영두절'이라고도 했다. 지금은 활동시간이 변화되어 8월 2일부터 10월 20일까지 매년 두 달 이상 지속되며 일년중 시간경과가 가장 큰 명절로서 마을마다 명절날자가 같지 않지만 내용은 비슷하다. 뜀머리를 연 마을에서는 집집마다 돼지와 소를 잡아 잔치를 벌였다. 민간에서는 어느 집이 손님을 가장 많이 초청했고 어느 집이 그 해에 가장 운이 좋았기 때문에 온 마을 사람들 외에 이웃 마을과 외지의 한족, 장족 군중들도 와서 참가했다.

跳岭头的基本程式是设傩坛、开傩坛、跳日午、捉傩妖。传统节目可以归纳为"安坛开光","歌舞娱乐","收妖封坛"三部分。表演以豆鼓为伴奏乐器,跳与唱分开,在舞的基础上融入民间杂耍和武术,叙事完整,唱词诙谐风趣,人物形象鲜明。舞师根据舞段的角色穿戴相应的服饰和面具,表演带有角色个性的程式舞蹈。傍晚时分班首主持"开坛"仪式后,舞师连续表演"扯大红、跳三师、跳师郎、跳忠相、操兵、跳四帅、抛云梯、跳仙姑"等舞段。经过通宵达旦的表演,最后跳"收精、赶龙船"舞段象征性地把代表邪魔、瘟疫的精头收尽在纸糊的龙船里,送到河边烧掉,表示从此灾害随水流逝,昭示吉祥安康。旧时的跳岭头,宗教祭祀成分较多,如今,跳岭头祭祀活动渐淡,娱乐气氛渐浓,师公们的酬神、歌唱、跳舞,在人们的眼中变成了一般的娱乐戏剧表演。"

The basic program of Tiao Lingtou consists of setting up Nuo altar, opening the altar, dancing at noon and chasing Nuo demons. The traditional programs can be summarized into three parts: "The opening of an altar", "the entertainment of singing and dancing", and "catching demons and sealing the altar". During the performance, Dou drum is played as the accompaniment instrument, dance and singing are separated, and folk juggling and martial arts are also incorporated. It also has complete narration, witty lyrics and distinctive characters. In the old days, there were more religious features in Tiao Lingtou, but nowadays, the ritual traits are weakening, while it is more of entertainment. The dancers wear costumes and masks according to the roles of the dance segment, perform a styled dance with the character's personality. In the evening, after the opening ceremony presided by the head of the troupe, the dancers perform a series of dances, including "Pulling the Red, Three-People Dancing, Teacher Dancing, Dancing for the loyal, Training the soldiers, Four-Generals Dancing, Throwing the Scaling Ladder, Fairy Dancing" and so on. After an all-night performance, the dancers finally perform the dance of "subduing evil spirit and driving off dragon boat", which symbolizes closing evil spirits and plagues in a paper dragon boat and sending it to the river for burning, indicating that the disaster will be drained with water, and good luck and well-being will be brought.

넘령두의 기본 프로그램은 나단(羅壇)을 설치하고, 개나단(开나단), 나일(낮)을 추고, 요괴를 잡는 것이다. 전통 프로그램은 '안티카이광

(安田開光)', '가무오락 (歌舞)', '요괴를 거두어 단을 봉함(封壇)' 세 부분으로 요약할 수 있다. 공연은 콩고를 반주악기로 하고 춤과 노래를 구별하며 무용의 기초우에 민간잡기와 무술을 융합시켜 서사가 완정하고 가사가 해학적이며 인물형상이 선명하다.무용사는 무용단의 배역에 따라 상응한 복식과 가면을 착용하고 그 배역의 개성이 담긴 양식무용을 선보인다. 저녁 무렵, 분수가 '개단' 의식을 진행한 후, 무사는 연속해서 '대홍을 뽑고, 삼사를 추고, 사랑을 추고, 충상을 추고, 조병을 뽑고, 사수를 추고, 고사를 던지고' 등의 춤을 선보였다. 밤새도록 공연을 한 후, 마지막에 춤을 추는 "정수를 거두어 용선을 쫓다"는 춤은 상징적으로 악마와 역병을 대표하는 정단의 머리를 모두 종이칠한 용선에 거두어 강가에 태워, 이로부터 재해가 물과 함께 흘러간다는 것을 상징하고, 상서롭고 평안함을 알렸다. 옛날에는 종교적인 제사 성분이 비교적 많았는데, 오늘날에는 제사 활동이 점차 줄어들고 오락의 분위기가 점점 짙어져, 스승과 공인들의 신에게 보답하는 것, 노래하고 춤은 사람들의 눈에는 일반적인 오락적인 연극 공연으로 변했다.'

"跳岭头"以民间信仰为依托,吸纳和展示丰富的民族民间歌舞、戏剧等文化元素,融节日习俗、信仰习俗、村社习俗、宗教习俗、娱乐习俗为一体,具有较高的学术价值;它源于壮族本土文化,同时吸收了汉族节日文化,是壮、汉民族文化交流与融合的产物,对促进民族大团结与文化交流有着十分重要的价值。

Based on folk beliefs, "Tiao Lingtou" absorbs and manifests rich cultural elements, such as folk songs, dances, and dramas.

It integrates customs in terms of festival, belief, village, religion, and entertainment, which are of great academic value. Originating from the local culture of the Zhuang Ethnic Group and absorbing the festival culture of the Han group, it is the product of cultural communication and integration between the two groups, playing significant role in promoting national unity and cultural exchange.

'넘령두'는 민간신앙을 바탕으로 풍부한 민족 민속 가무, 연극 등 문화요소를 흡수하고 전시하며 명절풍속, 신앙풍속, 마을풍속, 종교풍속, 오락풍속을 일체화시켜 비교적 높은 학술가치가 있다. 이는 쫭족의 본토문화에서 기원한 동시에 한족의 명절문화를 받아들여 쫭족과 한족의 문화교류와 융합의 산물로서 민족대단결과 문화교류를 촉진하는데 매우 중요한 가치가 있다.

27. 壮族霜降节

Frost's Descent Festival of Zhuang Ethnic Group

[入选时间：2014　Time: 2014

遗产名录：第四批国家级非物质文化遗产扩展项目名录

Heritage Category: Extended list of the fourth batch of National Intangible Cultural Heritage.

地域：崇左　Region: Chongzuo]

壮族霜降节是广西一个富有地方特色的节庆文化，一般在每年阳历的 10 月 24 日左右的霜降节气期间，壮语里称的"旦那"（即晚稻收割结束）之后。从霜降节举办的时间看，霜降节还与稻作族群的节期规律有关，是丰收节的一种形式。主要流行于大新、天等、德保、靖西、那坡等县的壮族德靖土语地区，其节日影响范围包括越南、云南、广西南宁、崇左等地区。这些地区每年都很重视这个独具特色的节日，对这个节日的热情不亚于中国的传统节日春节。

Frost's Descent Festival of Zhuang ethnic group is a local festival in Guangxi, which is usually celebrated around October 24 in the Frost Descent solar term of China, the frosty period after "Danna" (the end of late rice harvest) in the Zhuang language. The time of Frost's Descent Festival is related to the regularity of the rice farming, and it is a form of harvest festival. It is mainly popular in the Dejing native speaking areas of the Zhuang Ethnic Group in Daxin, Tiandeng, Debao, Jingxi, Napo and other counties. Its influence spreads into Nanning and Chongzuo of Guangxi, Yunnan province, and even Vietnam, where great importance is attached to this unique festival every year and the enthusiasm for this festival is no less than Spring Festival.

서리강강절은 광시성의 지역특색이 강한 축제문화로서 일반적으로 매년

양력 10월 24일을 서리강강절기기간으로 장어에서 "단나"(늦벼수확이 끝난 뒤)라고 한다. 상강절은 또 벼재배군체의 계절법칙과도 관계되는 풍작절의 한 형식이다. 주로 다신, 톈둥, 더바오, 징시, 나포 등 현의 쫭족 더징토어 지역에서 유행하며, 그 명절의 영향 범위는 베트남, 윈난, 광시 난닝, 충좌 등 지역을 포함한다. 이들 지역에서는 매년이 특색있는 명절을 중시하며 중국의 전통 명절인 춘절 못지않은 열정을 보이고 있다.

由于壮族地区特殊地理位置和悠久的土司文化，霜降节由单纯庆丰收的节庆活动发展成为祭祀民族英雄、进行商贸活动、民俗文化表演的综合性民俗活动。霜降节庆祝活动持续三天，分为"初降"（或称头降）、"正降"与"收降"（或称尾降），传统上的正降日这天上午为敬神活动，人们拿着糍粑、猪肉、香烛等祭品到娅莫庙祭拜进香迎神。之后进行游神活动，青年男子打扮成士兵模样，举着牙旗，敲锣打鼓，在狮子的开道下把女英雄娅莫画像抬出来巡游。娅莫像要挨家挨户地巡游，巡到哪家，哪家就要放鞭炮。游神活动结束后，节庆活动即进入"霜降圩"，人们在霜降节期间购买生产用具和生活用品，为第二年的春耕做准备。现在的霜降节和以前的大不一样，现在的霜降节在注重纪念英雄外，更注重商品的贸易。

Due to the special geographical location and long-standing chieftain culture of the Zhuang area, Frost's Descent Festival has developed from a simple harvest festival activity to a comprehensive folk custom activity of offering sacrifices to national heroes, conducting business activities and performing folk culture. Frost's Descent Festival celebration lasts for three days, and consists of "before descending" (or head descent), "descending" and "after descending" (or tail descent). Traditionally on the morning of descending day, people perform God worship activities, carrying Ciba (glutinous rice cake), pork, incense and other offerings to Yamo Temple for worship. After that, young men dressed as soldiers, holding the flag of the ancient local government, beating drums, and carrying the portrait of Yamo to parade in the path of lion players. Yamo portrait is paraded from house to house, and firecrackers are set off when her portrait arrived at every house. After that, the festival will come to the "Frost's Descent Fair", during which people buy products and daily necessities to prepare for the spring ploughing and cultivation in the following year. The current Frost's Descent Festival is very different from the previous one. In addition to commemorate the hero, the festival also pays more attention to the trade of commodities.

Yamo: a woman hero fighting for the country and the story to memorize her is regarded as one of the origin stories of Frost Descent Festival.

좡족지역의 특수한 지리적 위치와 유구한 토사 문화로 인해 상강절은 단순히 풍년을 경축하던 행사로부터 민족 영웅에게 제사 지내고 상업무역활동, 민속문화공연을 진행하는 종합적인 민속활동으로 발전하였다. 상강절 경축 활동은 3일간 진행되며, "초강"(혹은 두강), "정강", "수강"(혹은 미강)으로 나뉜다. 전통적으로 정강일에는 찹쌀 바, 돼지고기, 향 등 제물을 들고 야모(夜모묘)에 가서 제사를 지내고 향을 피워 신을 맞이한다. 후에 신령놀이(神神놀이)가 진행되었는데, 병사모습으로 분장한 청년들이 아기를 들고 꽹과리를 치고 북을 두드리며 사자의 길 아래 여영웅 야모(雅모)의 초상화를 들고 순시하였다. 야모는 집집마다 순회하면서 어느 집집마다 폭죽을 터뜨리려 했다. 성우놀이가 끝나면 명절행사가 열리는 '상강우'에 들어서는데 사람들은 상강절에 생산용구와 생활용품을 구입하여 이듬해의 봄갈이를 준비한다. 지금의 상강절은 이전의 절과는 크게 다르다. 현재의 상강절은 영웅을 기념하는 것 외에 상품의 무역을 더욱 중시한다.

除了商品贸易活动外，壮族霜降节更是文化展演的大舞台。正降日晚上，进入丰富多彩的文体活动时间。人们搭起舞台，开演土戏（壮戏），年轻人则三三两两地对起山歌，对歌活动一直持续到第二天的尾降，形成规模宏大的霜降歌圩。传统的霜降节都有舞龙舞狮、斗鸡耍猴、对歌唱土戏等活动。现在的霜降节，在企业的赞助下，政府和当地社区还组织篮球赛、拔河比赛、山歌比寒等娱乐活动，使得壮族霜降节活动更是精采纷呈。

In addition to commodity trade activities, Frost's Descent Festival of Zhuang ethnic group is also a large stage for cultural performances. On the evening of Frost Descend day, colorful cultural and sports activities are performed. People set up a stage to perform local opera (Zhuang opera), and young people sang folk songs in pairs and threes. The singing activity lasted until the end of the second day, forming a famous "Frost's Descent Song Fair". The traditional Frost's Descent festival has many activities, such as dragon and lion dances, cockfights and monkey tricks and singing local opera. In current Frost's Descent Festival, under the sponsorship of enterprises, the government and local communities also organize entertainment activities such as basketball games, tug-of-war matches, and folk song competitions, making the Zhuang Frost's Descent Festival activities more wonderful.

상품무역활동외에도 좡족상강절은 문화전시공연의 큰 무대이다. 정강일 저녁은 풍부하고 다채로운 문체활동시간으로 들어간다. 사람들은 무대를 설치하고 토극 (웅장한 희극)을 공연하면 젊은이들은 삼삼오오로 산노래를 주고 받았다. 이 노래는 이튿날이 끝날 때까지 지속되어 규모가 거대한 서리강가장을 이루었다. 전통 상강절에는 모두 용사자춤 · 닭싸움 · 원숭이놀이 · 대가창 · 토극 등의 활동이 있다. 현재는 기업의 후원하에 정부와 지역사회에서 농구경기, 줄다리기, 산노래비한 등 오락활동을 조직하여 좡족 서리강하절 행사를 더욱 다채롭게 만들어 가고 있다.

28. 壮族三月三

March 3rd Festival of Zhuang Ethnic Group
[入选时间：2014 Time: 2014
遗产名录：第四批国家级非物质文化遗产扩展项目名录
Heritage Category: Extended list of the fourth batch of National Intangible Cultural Heritage.
地域： 南宁　Region: Nanning]

壮族三月三主要流传于广西中南部的武鸣县境，以武鸣县的城厢镇、两江镇等乡镇为核心区域，覆盖到武鸣县周边如隆安、上林、宾阳、马山等县，辐射到全广西乃至广东、云南、贵州等省份的壮族聚居地区。

March 3rd Festival of Zhuang is most originated in Wuming County in middle-eastern Guangxi Autonomous Region, of which Chengxiang town and Liangjiang town are the core birthplaces of the festival. Gradually, its celebration extended to the neighboring counties in Guangxi such as Long'an, Shanglin, Binyang and Mashan and even radiated to outer residential communities in such provinces as Guangdong, Yunnan and Guizhou where Zhuang people inhabit. Nowadays,

좡족 3월 3일은 주로 광시 중남부의 우밍현 경내에서 전파되며, 우밍현의 청샹진, 량쟝진 등 향진을 핵심 지역으로 하며, 우밍현 주변의 룽안, 상림, 빈양, 마산 등 현에까지 미치고, 광시 전 나아가 광동, 운남, 구이저우 등 성의 좡족 집거 지역까지 전파된다.

农历三月三是中国多个民族的传统节日，其中以壮族、苗族、瑶族为典型。在古代被称为上巳节，在这一天人们纷纷来到水边举行祭礼，洗濯去垢，消除不祥，被称为祓禊。也有的地方在三月三拜祖先、拜轩辕、拜蚩尤。在壮族传说中，三月三是壮族始祖布洛陀诞辰日，因此农历三月三也是壮族祭祖、祭拜布洛陀始祖的重要日子。传统壮族三月三的重要内涵是祈求物的丰产和人的丰产，习俗活动首先是敬神祈丰，这些神灵包括真武、花婆、祖神、村寨神等。在祭祀之后，随之会有聚餐、对歌、唱戏、抢花炮、抛绣球等娱乐活动。

March 3rd Festival (the third day of March in Chinese lunar calendar) is a traditional Chinese ethnic festival typically observed among ethnic groups of Zhuang, Miao and Yao. It is known as Shangsi Festival in ancient times, when people came to the river for a ritual cleansing to eliminate evil spirits, also known as Fuxi. There are also some places on March 3rd holding a serial outdoor activities to worship their ancestors and others like Xuanyuan and Chiyou. According to the legends of Zhuang people, it is the birthdate of Buluotuo, the creator god of Zhuang. worship Xuanyuan, worship Chiyou. In Zhuang legend, the third day of March is the birthday of Buluotuo, the first ancestor of the Zhuang people. Therefore, March 3rd is also an important day for Zhuang people to worship their ancestors and worship Buluotuo. The important connotation of the traditional March 3rd of Zhuang people is to pray for the fertility of things and people. The previous traditional activities are characterized to pray for fertility and worship the gods including Zhenwu, Huapo, ancestor god, village god and so on. After the sacrifice, there will be feast, singing in antiphonal style, opera performance, grabbing Huapao (a special kind of firecracker) and throwing embroidered silk balls and other entertainment activities.

Xuanyuan(轩辕): the personal name of Yellow Emperor in Chinese ancient legend, who was the first emperor and leader of china.

Chiyou (蚩尤): a tribal leader of the Nine Li tribe (九黎) in ancient China, who is best known as a king who lost against the future Yellow Emperor during the Three Sovereigns and Five Emperors era in Chinese mythology.

음력 3월 3일은 중국 여러 민족의 전통 명절인데 좡족, 묘족, 요족이 대표적이다. 고대에는 상사절(上巳节) 이라고 했는데, 이 날에 사람들은 잇달아 물가에 가서 제례를 지내고, 때를 씻어 상서롭지 못한 것을 없애는 것을 상재라고 했다. 어떤 곳에서는 3월 3일에 조상에게 절을 하고 헌원에게 절을 하며 치우에게 절을 하기도 한다. 좡족 전설에서 3월 3일은 좡족의 시조인 브로다 탄신일이기 때문에 음력 3월 3일은 좡족이 시조에게 제사를 지내고 브로다 시조에게 제사를 지내는 중요한 날이다. 전통 좡족 3월 3일의 중요한 내용은 물품과 사람의 풍작을 기원하는 것이다. 풍속 활동은 우선 신을 섬기며 풍작을 비는 것인데, 이러한 신령에는 진무(眞武) · 화파(花파) · 조신(祖神) · 마을신(村神) 등이 있다. 제사 후에 회식, 노래 맞대기, 희극 부르기, 화포 빼앗기, 공 던지기 등의 오락이 뒤따른다.

五色糯米饭是壮族人们在三月三期间制作用于祭祖祭神、赶歌圩之用,在节前家家户户准备五色糯米饭,用红兰草、黄饭花、枫叶、紫蕃藤等植物的汁浸泡糯米,做成红、黄、黑、紫、白五色糯米饭。相传,这种食品是深得仙女们的赞赏后流传下来的,也有人说是祭祀歌仙刘三姐的。

Five-color glutinous rice is made by Zhuang people during March 3rd Festival and it is served in ancestors and gods worship as well as song fairs. Before the festival, every household prepares five-color glutinous rice by extracting colors of red, yellow, black, and purple from certain plants to dye the rice. Some people said that five-color glutinous rice was circulated after winning the praise of the Goddess in heaven, while others reckon it as a memory of the singing goddess, Liu Sanjie.

명절이 다가오면 집집마다 오색 찹쌀밥을 준비한다. 찹쌀을 적란초, 노랑밥꽃, 단풍잎, 자번 등 식물 즙에 담가 적황색, 흑색, 자색, 백색으로 만든다. 전하는데 의하면 이 음식은 선녀들의 상찬을 받은 후 전해지고 있으며 가선 유삼저를 제사지낸다는 설도 있다.

歌圩是壮族三月三的主要活动,男女青年对唱山歌,进行社交和文娱活动。方圆数十里内的男女青年聚集在歌圩点,小伙子在歌师的指点下与中意的姑娘对歌。此外，彩蛋则是歌圩中男女青年用以交际传达情感的物品。随着社会的发展，壮族三月三的内容不断扩大，尤其是壮族三月三期间的对歌活动成为显性的内容，聚会交友、商品贸易等活动获得强化。

The song fair is the main activity of the Zhuang people on March 3rd. Young men and women sing folk songs together for social and recreational activities.Young men and women from dozens of miles around gathered at the singing site where boys would sing in antiphonal style with the girls they like under the guidance of the song master. In addition, colored eggs are used for young men and women to convey their emotions during song fairs. With the development of society, the celebrating practices of the Zhuang people's March 3rd are constantly expanded in which the song fair activities, gathering, making friends and commodity trading are dominant.

노래장은 쫭족들이 3월 3일에 하는 주요한 활동으로서 남녀청년들이 함께 산가를 부르면서 사교와 문화오락활동을 진행하였다. 주변 수십리 안의 남녀 청년들이 노래장에 모였는데 젊은이는 노래장의 지도를 받아 마음에 드는 처녀들과 노래를 대주었다. 이외에 채단이란 노래장에서 남녀청년들이 교제하면서 정감을 전달하는 물품이다. 사회가 발전함에 따라 쫭족 3월 3일 (三月三日)의 내용은 끊임없이 확대되었으며, 특히 쫭족 3월 3일 (三月三) 기간의 듀엣 활동은 지배적인 내용이 되었고, 모임

교제, 상품 무역 등의 활동도 강화되었다.

壮族三月三期间广西一些少数民族地区的民间也会组织一些体育竞技活动。抢花炮活动在三江侗族自治县等地还颇为隆重，传统的"花炮"是一个铁制圆环，直径约5厘米，外用红布或红绸缠绕，主持人点上火药放炮，将红炮圈射上高空，炮圈落下时各队的选手争先抢夺，规则类似于西方的橄榄球运动，故被称为"东方橄榄球"。隆林各族自治县在三月三期间还开展一项叫"踩风车"的体育竞技活动。

During March 3rd Festival, some folk sports competitions will be organized in some minority areas of Guangxi. Grabbing Huapao in Sanjiang Dong Autonomous County and other places is quite an important local event. The traditional Huapao is made of a round iron circle about 5cm in diameter and wrapped with red cloth or silk. While playing the host ignited the Huapao and casted it to sky, then the players would jostle to grab it when it falls down. It has similar rules of rugby thus earns the name "Oriental Rugby". Longlin Autonomous County also holds sports competition called "stepping on windmills" during March 3rd.

장족 3월 3일이 기간에 광서의 일부 소수민족지구의 민간에서도 일부

체육경기 활동을 조직한다. 화포빼앗기활동은 삼강동족자치현 등지에서도 매우 성대하였다. 전통적인 "화포"는 철제 원, 직경 약 5cm, 바깥은 붉은 천 또는 붉은 비단으로 싸여, 진행자가 화약을 점화하여 대포를 터뜨리고, 붉은 포 원을 하늘 높이 발사한다, 포 원이 떨어질 때 각 팀의 선수들이 먼저 빼앗는다. 규칙이 서양의 럭비와 비슷해서, "동양 럭비"라고 불린다. 룽린 각 민족 자치현은 3월 3일 기간에 '풍차 밟기'라는 체육 경기 활동도 펼친다.

2014 年, 壮族三月三成为广西地方性法定节假日, 广西壮族自治区 政府加大了对壮族 三月三的 宣传推广和组织工作, 每年三月三期 间都会举办一系列形式新、立意高、群众参与度高的活动, 吸引着全国各地的游客。" 三月三"已经从一个传统民族节日发展到文化旅游节庆, 也成了广西当地的文旅品牌, 成为跨族群、跨地区的民族节庆活动。

In 2014, March 3rd Festival of Zhuang is authorized as a local holiday of Guangxi. Local government of Guangxi Zhuang Autonomous has been strengthening its publicity, promotion and organization. Every year Guangxi would hold a series of activities which are innovative, meaningful, and high-participative during March 3rd Festival, attracting nation-wide tourists. Now, the festival has been developed into a culture-tourism day with cross-ethnic and cross-region activities as well as an authentic culture-tourism brand of Guangxi from a traditional ethnic holiday.

2014년 좡족 3월 3일은 광서 지방성 법정 공휴일로 되었다. 광서**좡족**자치구 정부는 광족 3월 3일에 대한 홍보와 조직 업무를 강화했으며 매년 3월 3일 기간에는 일련의 형식이 새롭고 취지가 높으며 대중참여도가 높은 활동을 개최하여 전국 각지의 관광객들을 끌어들이고 있다. '삼월삼'은 이미 전통 민족 명절에서 문화 관광 축제로 발전했으며 광시 현지의 문화 관광 브랜드가 되었고 다민족 군, 다지역 민족 행사가 되었다.

29. 中元节（资源河灯节）

Ziyuan River Latern Festival

[入选时间：2014　Time: 2014

遗产名录：第四批国家级非物质文化遗产扩展项目名录

Heritage Category: Extended list of the fourth batch of National Intangible Cultural Heritage.

地域：桂林　Region: Guilin]

资源河灯节是流传于广西壮族自治区桂林市资源县的资源镇、中峰乡、梅溪乡一带极具民族特色和地域特色的传统节日,它是依附中元节形成和存在的。

Ziyuan River Lantern Festival is a traditional festival with particularly strong ethnic and local features, emerging as a derivative form of Hungry Ghost Festival. It is popular among areas of Ziyuang town, Zhongfeng township, and Meixi township in Guilin city, Guangxi Zhuang Autonomous Region.

자원하등축제는 광시좡족자치구 계림시 자원현의 자원진, 중펑향, 메이시향 일대에서 민족특색과 지역특색을 지닌 전통명절로서 중원절에 의지하여 형성되고 존재하였다.

每当七月半中元节,人们都会自发地为葬身资江的冤魂做道场超度,末了放几盏河灯,一来以示对亡者的祭奠,二来也求自身辟邪消灾,万事大吉。后由湖南会馆在中元之夜统一组织民众漂放河灯,相沿成俗便形成了今天的河灯节。

On Hungry Ghost Festival, which takes place every year on the evening of the 15th day of Ghost Month, the 7th month on the lunar calendar, people would spontaneously held rituals for the deceased who had been wrongfully killed and jumped into the Ziyuan river to release from purgatory. Before completing the rituals, people would put some lanterns on the surface of the river, in order to pay their tribute to the deceased and warding off evil spirits and disasters to wish all the best. Later on Hunan Guild Hall organized people to release lanterns onto the river at the night of the Hungry Ghost day and the customs handed down, forming today's River Lantern Festival.

매번 7월 6일 중원절이면 사람들은 자발적으로 자강 (子江)에 묻힌 원혼을 위해 도장 (道章)을 행하며 마지막에는 강등을 몇 개 올려 망자에 대한 제사를 지내고 둘째는 자신의 악함을 물리치고 재화를 제거하며 만사대길하기를 바란다. 후에 호남 회관에서는 중원날 밤에 통일적으로 민중을 조직하여 강등을 드리우게 하였는데 점차 풍속이 형성되어, 오늘의 강등축제가 형성되었다.

起初,资源河灯只有"敬神灯""莲花灯""粽子灯"三种。河灯有指路照明的意思,寓意着给游荡在外的游魂照亮引导归家之路。"敬神灯"以四根灯柱打成一个框架,四面糊透光皮纸贴上吉语,用来敬河神,祈求河神佑护免遭覆舟之灾。"莲花灯"则以剪成莲花状的彩纸糊于一个碗周,似盛开的莲花,取佛教的莲花洁净之意,作超度魂灵之用。随着河灯的制作工艺及内容得以日益完善和丰富,河灯的种类也丰富多样,如龙灯、鱼灯、彩灯等等,寄寓着人们对美好生活的希望。以河灯为主体内涵的资源河灯节渐成规模,形成了一个以祭祖、祈福、商贸、民娱等内容为主的地方性节庆。

At the beginning, there were only three different types of Ziyuan river lanterns, including the god-worship lantern, the lotus flower lantern, and the Zongzi lantern. The river lantern has a meaning of indicating the road and lighting, suggesting that the lantern lights the way home for the wandering ghosts. The god-worship lantern is made in the shape of a frame fixed by four lighting poles and pasted with transparent leather paper with auspicious words written on it. The lantern is used to worship the River God for protecting their boats from getting overturned. The lotus flower lantern is made by pasting around a bowl with lotus flower-shaped color paper. Looking like a blooming lotus flower, it contains the meaning of Buddhism purity from and used for releasing souls from purgatory. When the craftsmanship of the river lantern improved, various lanterns have also emerged, such as the dragon lantern, the fish lantern, and the color lantern, which carry people's hopes for a better life. The Ziyuan River Lantern Festival, centered on the river lanterns, is gradually taking shape as a local festival mainly containing ancestor worship, praying for blessings, business, and recreation.

당초 자원하 등은 경신등, 연꽃등, 쫑쯔등 등 3 종류만 있었다. 강등(河燈)은 길을 밝히는 조명이라는 의미가 있는데 밖에서 떠도는 혼령에게 귀갓길을 밝혀준다는 뜻이다. 경신등(敬神燈)은 4개의 기둥으로 하나의 틀을 만들고, 4 면을 투명한 가죽 종이로 상서로운 말을 붙여, 강의 신을 존경하고, 배가 전복되는 재난을 면하도록 강의 신에게 기도하는 데 사용한다. '연등'은 연꽃 모양으로 오린 채색종이를 사발에 붙여 마치 활짝 핀 연꽃처럼 만들어 붙이는 것으로, 불교의 연꽃이 청결하다는 의미에서 혼령을 섬기는 데 쓰인다. 강등의 제작공예와 내용이 날로 완벽해지고 풍부해짐에 따라 강등의 종류도 다양해졌는데 이를테면 용등, 어등, 채등 등은 사람들의 아름다운 생활에 대한 희망을 담고 있다. 강등(河灯)을 주체로 하는 자원 강등축제는 점차 규모를 형성하여 조상제사, 기원복, 상업, 오락 등 내용을 위주로 하는 지방성축제로 되였다.

30. 桂剧

Gui Opera

[入选时间：2006 Time: 2006

遗产名录：第一批国家级非物质文化遗产名录

Heritage Category: List of the first batch of National Intangible Cultural Heritage.

地域： 南宁　Region: Nanning]

桂剧是广西主要的地方剧种，原称"桂林戏"、"桂班戏"，属皮黄戏系统。流布于桂北、桂中、桂东北和桂西北的桂林市、柳州市、贺州市、河池市和梧州市辖区以及湘南近六十个市、县，其中尤以桂林市、柳州市等"官话"地区最为盛行。

Gui Opera is the main local opera in Guangxi. It was originally called "Guilin opera" and "Guiban opera", belonging to the Pihuang opera system. It spreads in Guilin, Liuzhou, Hezhou, Hechi and Wuzhou districts of Guangxi, as well as nearly 60 cities and counties in southern Hunan, among which Guilin, Liuzhou and other "Mandarin" areas are most prevalent.

계극(桂劇)은 광시의 주요한 지방 연극 종류로, 원래는 '계림희(桂林戏)', '계반희(桂版戏)'라고 불렀으며, 피황희(皮黄戏) 계통이다. 구이베이, 구이중, 구이시 동북부와 구이시 서북의 계림, 류저우, 허저우, 허츠, 우저우 관할 및 샹난 남부의 근 60개시·현에 분포하고 있으며, 계림시, 류저우시 등 '관화'지역이 가장 성행한다.

桂剧历史比较悠久，大约发端于明代中叶，明末清初昆腔流播到广西，后高腔和弋阳腔又相继传入，几种声腔相互融合形成桂剧。桂剧做工细腻贴切、生动活泼，借助面部表情和身段姿态传情，注重以细腻而富于生活气息的表演手法塑造人物。

Gui Opera originated in mid-Ming Dynasty. In late Ming and early Qing dynasties, Kunqiang was spread to Guangxi, and then Gaoqiang and Yiyangqiang were introduced one after another. These tunes merged and formed the Gui Opera, which is exquisite, appropriate and lively. It conveys emotions with facial expressions and body posture, and emphasizes the portrayal of characters with exquisite and life-like performance techniques.

계극은 력사가 비교적 유구한바 명조중엽부터 시작되었고 명조말기와 청조초기에 곤강(昆腔)이 광서에 전파되였으며, 후에는 익양강(익양강)과 고강(高腔)이 잇달아 전해지면서 몇 가지 곡조가 서로 융합되여 계극을 형성하였다. 계극은 작품이 섬세하고 절묘하며 생동하고 활발하며 얼굴표정과 자태를 이용하여 감정을 표현하고 섬세하고 생활분위기가 풍부한 연기수법으로 인물을 형상화하는데 중점을 두고 있다.

桂剧传统剧目丰富，有"大小本杂八百出"之说。由于它的产生和发展与徽剧、汉剧、湘剧、祁剧都有着密切的血缘关系，所以它的剧目多与皮黄系统的兄弟剧种相似。道光、咸丰年间，祁剧传入。由于戏路接近、语音相似，祁、桂艺人长期同台、同剧演出，使桂剧声腔、演技深受影响，发展日臻成熟。

The traditional repertoire of Gui Opera has the saying that

"there are eight hundred books of different sizes", which shows the large number of the opera. Since its emergence and development are closely related to Anhui Opera, Han Opera, Xiang Opera and Qi Opera, its repertoire is mostly similar to the Pihuang opera system. During the period of Emperor Daoguang and Xianfeng, Qi Opera was introduced to Guangxi. Because of the proximity and similar pronunciation of the two operas, Qi and Gui artists performed on the same stage for a long time, which greatly affected the tunes and acting skills of Gui Opera and contributed to its development.

계극은 전통적인 레퍼토리가 풍부하여 '대소본 잡팔백출'이라는 설이 있다. 그 출현과 발전은 휘극, 한극, 상극, 기극 등과 밀접한 혈연관계를 갖고 있기에 그 레퍼토리는 대부분 피황계통의 형제극종과 비슷하다. 도광(道光)과 함풍(咸風) 연간에 기극(奇劇)이 도입되었다. 연극 노선이 가깝고 어음이 비슷하기 때문에 기(基)와 구이예(桂藝)는 장기간 같은 무대에 같은 극으로 공연하여 구이극의 곡조와 연기가 깊은 영향을 받아 발전이 날로 원숙해졌다.

桂剧用桂林方言演唱, 声调优美, 抑扬有致。在唱腔方面, 桂剧有高、弹、昆、吹腔及杂腔小调, 以弹腔为主; 高腔属弋阳腔派系, 现存唱腔曲牌数百支, 音乐特点突出, 极具风韵; 昆腔属湘昆派系, 别具一格; 吹腔音乐唱腔幽默风趣, 自成一体; 杂腔小调与本地民歌曲调紧密结合, 极具生活情趣。桂剧乐队伴奏分为文、武场,文场使用"三大件"等,武场则为锣鼓打击乐,以高边锣、星子锣较有特色。

Performing in Guilin dialect, Gui Opera is melodious and well-regulated. In terms of singing, Gui Opera has tunes of Gaoqiang, Tanqiang, Kunqiang, Chuiqiang and miscellaneous minor tunes, but most falls on Tanqiang. Gaoqiang belongs to the faction of the Yiyangqiang, with hundreds of tune names existed. It is outstanding in musical characteristics and has a great charm. Kunqiang is unique and belongs to Hunan and kunshan factions. Chuiqiang is humorous in singing and has a style of its own. The miscellaneous minor tunes is closely integrated with the local folk songs, which is full of fun in life. The band accompaniment is divided into Wenchang and Wuchang. The former is dominated by "Three major pieces", while Wuchang uses gongs and drums for percussion music, featuring in Gaobian gongs and Xingzi gongs.

계극은 계림방언으로 노래하는데 성조가 아름답고 억양이 운치가 있다. 곡조 방면에서 계극은고 (高), 탄 (탄), 곤 (곤), 취조 (曲調) 및 잡조 (雜調) 단조가 있고 탄조 (炭調)를 위주로 한다. 고조는 익양강 (익양강) 계파에 속하며 현존하는 곡조곡패 수백수가 있는데 음악특점이 두드러지고 멋이 있다. 곤강은 상곤파별로서 남다른 풍격을 가지고 있었다. 취강음악은 곡조가 유모아적이고 해학적이며 서로 일체감을 이룬다. 잡강단조는 현지 민요곡조와 긴밀히 결합되여 생활의 정취를 띠고 있다. 계극악단의 반주는 문 (文), 무장 (武場), 문장 (文場)은 '3대 기물' 등을 사용한다. 무장은 쟁과리, 북, 타악을 사용하는데 고변징 (高변징), 별자징 (星子쟁과리)이 비교적 특색이 있다.

桂剧在表演方面有马步、跳台、摆刀、跳加官等表演程式。脚色分为生、旦、净、丑四大行当。生行又分生、末、外、小、武；旦行中又分旦、占、贴、夫；净行则分为净、副、末净；丑得只分丑和小丑。同时，历代桂剧艺人还创造了许多表演特技，如"跌箱功""罗帽功""紫金冠功"以及净行各角色脸谱。

In terms of performance, Gui Opera has special performance programs such as Horse Stance, Platform Jumping, Broadsword Swinging, and Tiaojiaguan. The roles of Gui Opera are divided into four major types: Sheng (male role), Dan (female role), Jing (painted face) and Chou (clown). Sheng is also sub-divided into Sheng, Mo, Wai, Xiao, and Wu; Dan is further divided into Dan, Zhan, Tie, Fu; Jing is divided into Jing, Vice, Mo Jing; Chou is divided into Chou and clown. At the same time, the artists of the past generations of Gui Opera have also created many special performances, such as "box dropping skills", "luo hat skills", "purple crown skills" and the facial makeup of each role in Jing.

Note: Three major pieces include Jinghu, Yueqin, and Sanxian. Jinghu is a two-stringed bowed instrument with a high register and also called Beijing opera fiddle. Yueqin is a four-stringed plucked instrument with a full-moon-shaped sound box. Sanxian is a three-stringed plucked instrument.

Tiaojiaguan is a dance style played before the performance is in progress and can be inserted with a simple ritual dance.

계극은 마보(馬步) · 도약대(뜀틀) · 나이프(나이프) · 뜀뛰기관(뜀뛰기) 등의 공연 프로그램이 있다. 발색은 생·단·정·추의 4대 직종으로 나뉜다. 출생행은 또 출생, 말, 외, 소, 무(武)로 나뉘며 단행(旦行)에서는 또 단(旦), 점(店), 단(丹), 부(夫)로 나뉜다. 정행(正行)은 정(正), 부(副), 말(末)으로 나뉜다. 못난 건 못난 사람과 어릿광대를 가릴 뿐이다. 한편, 역대 계극예술인들은 많은 특기를 만들어 냈는데, 예를 들면 '하상공', '라모공', '자금관공'과 각종 배역의 얼굴 분장을 모두 만들었다.

桂剧融会了广西特有的风土民情和人文特点，形成了细腻婉约、灵秀生动、刚柔并济、富有乡土气息的风格特色和贴近生活的质朴简约之美，是桂林地方文化遗产中的一个重要组成部分。

Integrating the unique local conditions, social customs and humanistic characteristics of Guangxi, Gui Opera gradually forms the local style of delicate and graceful, beautiful and vivid, rigid and flexible, and its simple beauty is very close to life. It is an important part of the local cultural heritage of Guilin.

구이극은 광시 특유의 풍토와 민정, 인문 특징을 융합하여 섬세하고 부드러우며, 향토적인 풍격 특색과 생활에 가까운 소박하고 간결한 미를 형성하였으며, 계림 지방 문화유산의 중요한 구성부분이다.

31. 桂南采茶戏

Guinan(South of Guangxi) Tea-picking Opera
[入选时间：2006 Time: 2006
遗产名录：第一批国家级非物质文化遗产名录
Heritage Category: List of the first batch of National Intangible Cultural Heritage.
地域： 玉林   Region: Yulin]

桂南采茶戏是广西汉族剧种戏曲之一，流传于广西南部的玉林市博白县及其周边地区的玉州、兴业、北流、陆川，以及相邻的钦州市部分地区，因其由小生、小旦、小丑为主演，故又称"三小戏"或"三角班"。

Guinan Tea-picking Opera is one of Han operas in Guangxi, which is prevailing in sothern regions of Guangxi, including Bobai County of Yulin and its surrounding areas such as Yuzhou, Xingye, Beiliu and Luchuan, and the adjacent parts of Qinzhou. It got the name "Three Roles Drama" or "Triangle Class" from the three main characters in the opera: Xiao Sheng (or Male role), Xiao Dan (or Female role) and Xiao Chou (or clown).

구이난 채차희(桂南 채차희)는 광시(廣西) 한족 희곡 중의 하나로, 광시 남부의 위린시 (玉林市) 박백현(博白縣)과 그 주변 지역인 위저우(玉州), 흥업(興業), 북류(北流), 루촨(陸川) 및 인접한 친저우(秦州) 일부 지역에 널리 보급되었으며, 소생(小生), 소단(小旦), 개그우(개그우)가 주연을 맡기 때문에 '삼소극(三小戏)' 혹은 '삼각반 (三小戏)'이라고도 한다.

桂南采茶戏于明末从江西赣南传入博白，距今已有四百多年的历史。由唱竹马发展为载歌载舞的唱采茶，清代已形成独特的表演风格，民国后逐步发展成熟，成为戏曲中的独立剧种。

Guinan Tea-picking Opera was introduced into Bobai from Southern Jiangxi province in late Ming Dynasty. It developed from Changzhuma[1] to tea-picking singing and dancing. In Qing Dynasty, a unique performance style was formed, and gradually gained its maturity in the late period of the Republic of China, which makes it an independent opera.

Note: Chang Zhuma: also named as hobby horse singing. There is an old saying that 'hobby horse into my home, and everyone is happy', which means that the hobby horse into the home, all the year round is smooth and profitable

계남채다희는 명나라 말기에 강서강서남부에서 박백에 전해져 들어왔는데 금으로부터 이미 400여년 전의 역사가 있다. "죽마춤"을 부르던데로부터 춤추고 차따기를 부르는 것으로 발전하였으며 청조때에 이미 독특한 공연풍격을 형성하였고 민국이후에 점차 발전, 성숙되어 희곡중의 독립적인 극종으로 되였다.

桂南采茶戏最初是以"十二月采茶"为主要内容的歌舞演唱，后在此基础上增加了开荒、点茶、探茶、采茶、炒茶、卖茶等情节，整个歌舞是通过种茶的全部劳动过程，反映劳动人民的劳动热情和丰收喜悦。

The main content of Guinan Tea-picking Opera was originally

based on the play "tea picking in December", which was previously about tea farmers' activities of twelve months in the whole year, and later developed into a whole set of songs and dances, such as clearing land, tea ordering, tea picking, tea frying, tea selling. These performances reflect the enthusiasm and joy of working people in the whole labor process of tea planting.

구이난 (桂南)의 차나무 희극은 최초에는 "12월에 차를 따다"를 주요 내용으로 하는 가무 공연이다가 후에 여기에 기초하여 황무지를 개간하고, 차를 따고, 차를 따고, 차를 볶고, 차를 파는 등의 줄거리를 추가하였으며, 전체 가무는 차를 재배하는 모든 노동 과정을 통해 노동 인민의 노동 열정과 풍년의 기쁨을 반영한다.

桂南采茶戏演出队伍精悍，机动灵活。队伍人数一般不超过10人，小道具、小节目，不受场地限制，演出方便。表演时通常由一人扮作茶公，两人扮作茶娘，桂南采茶戏的表演别具一格，载歌载舞，在歌舞中穿插一些有情节的生活小戏。包括唱念做舞四功，侧重于唱和舞，念白多数为韵白或骈文，演出气氛热烈，剧场效果良好。桂南采茶戏的乐器有击乐、器乐和道器。击乐包括锣、鼓、钹、木鱼；器乐包括唢呐、二胡、笛子、碰铃；道器包括钱鞭、彩带、花扇、手绢。

Guinan Tea-picking Opera performance team is capable and flexible, with no more than 10 members, small props, short programs, which makes it free of set restriction and performance limitation. During the performance, one person usually plays the role of tea master and another two as tea girls. In the song and dance, some plots of life are interspersed. The performance of Guinan Tea-picking Opera is unique and includes four skills of singing, chanting, acting and dancing, in which singing and dancing are emphasized. Most chanting parts are rhymical or parallel. The atmosphere of the performance is warm and effective. Percussion instruments, wind instruments and props are used in Guinan Tea-picking Opera. Percussion instruments include gongs, drums, cymbals, wooden knockers; wind instruments consist of suona, erhu, flute, and finger cymbals; props include coin whip (it is made of a bamboo pole or steel tube with 8~16 copper coins strung into each end after holes are pierced, and tied with five colored cloth strips), ribbon, flower fan and handkerchief.

계남 채차희 공연 대오는 민첩하고 민첩했다. 팀의 인원수는 일반적으로 10명을 넘지 않으며, 소도구, 소프로그램은 장소의 제한을 받지 않아 공연에 편리하다. 공연할 때 보통 한사람이 다공(茶公)으로 분장하고 두사람이 다낭(茶娘)으로 분장하는데 계남채다희는 독특한 풍격이 있어 노래하고 춤추며 노래속에 줄거리가 있는 생활극을 삽입한다. 창, 독, 무

4 공을 포함하는데 창과 무에 치중하고 념백은 대부분 운백 혹은 병문으로서 공연분위기가 열렬하고 극장효과가 좋다. 계남 채차희의 악기에는 타악, 기악과 도기가 있다. 타악에는 징·북·심벌즈·목어 등이 있다. 기악에는 수르나이, 얼후, 피리, 타종 등이 있고도 기로는 돈줄·채색 띠·화선·손수건이 있다.

桂南采茶戏具有浓厚的地方特色, 它与当地 群众的文化生活、审美情趣密不可分, 其保护和传承对丰富和完善中国戏曲乃至世界戏曲都具有一定的推动作用, 对丰富人民群众文化生活都具有很大的促进作用。

Guinan Tea-picking Opera has strong local characteristics, which are inseparable from the cultural life and aesthetic taste of the local people. Its protection and inheritance play a certain role in promoting the enrichment and improvement of Chinese opera and even the world opera, as well as in the enrichment of people's cultural life.

구이난(桂南)의 채차희극은 짙은 지방특색을 가지고 있다. 그것은 현지 대중의 문화생활, 심미 정취와 불가분의 관계가 있다. 보호와 전승은 중국 희곡 더 나아가서는 세계 희곡을 풍부히 하고 보완하는데 일정한 추진작용을 가지고 있다. 또한 인민 대중의 문화생활을 풍부히 하는데 매우 큰 촉진작용을 가지고 있다.

32. 壮族七十二巫调音乐

Zhuang Witch Songs with Seventy-two Tunes
[入选时间：2014 Time: 2014
遗产名录：第四批国家级非物质文化遗产名录
Heritage Category: List of the fourth batch of National Intangible Cultural Heritage.
地域：百色 Region: Baise]

壮族七十二巫调音乐是壮族女巫举行仪式时所唱的一种巫歌，也称巫论，壮语称"欢经"，主要流行于广西百色市凌云县境内的泗城镇。壮族七十二巫调是我国罕见的民族民间音乐调子群，是我国目前保留最完整的由巫文化逐步转化而来的原生态音乐。

Zhuang Witch Songs with Seventy-two Tunes is a witch song sung by Zhuang witches when they hold ceremonies. It is also called witchcraft theory, and "Huan Jing" in Zhuang dialect. It is mainly popular in Sicheng town, Lingyun county of Baise in Guangxi Zhuang Autonomous Region. It is a rare tune group of folk music in China and also the most complete original music in China which has been gradually developed from the witch culture.

좡족 72 무조음악은 좡족 무녀가 의식을 거행할 때 부르는 무가의 일종으로 무론이라고도 하며 좡족어로 '환경'이라고 한다. 주로 광시 바이서시 릉운현 경내의 쓰청시에서 유행된다. 좡족 72 무조는 중국에서 보기 드문 민족 민간음악 곡조군으로서 현재 우리나라에서 가장 완전하게 보존하고 있는 무당문화가 점차 전환되어 온 원래의 생태음악이다.

据考证，早在3000多年前，壮族先民就在凌云这片土地上刀耕火种、繁衍生息。在大自然面前，壮族先民显得渺小无力，男人们上山耕种和打猎往往一去不回，疾病和天灾也经常夺去人们的生命。壮族妇女为寄托哀思、缓解悲痛、避免灾难、抒发理想，在长期的生产生活中逐渐形成了壮族七十二巫调音乐。

It is proved that the ancestors of the Zhuang people had already cultivated and lived in Lingyun as early as 3000 years ago. Compared with the force of nature, Zhuang ancestors of are quite powerless. At that time, men often lost their lives while going out for farming and hunting in the mountains, and diseases and natural disasters often took away people's lives. Zhuang women sung the Witch Songs in order to relieve their grief, pray to avoid disasters and express their dreams. Zhuang Witch Songs with Seventy-two Tunes has gradually come into being in Zhuang people's daily life and production activities.

고증에 따르면 3000여 년 전에 좡족 선민들은 릉운이라는 이 땅에서 화전을 경작하며 생활했다. 대자연앞에서 좡족선조들은 보잘 것 없고 무력하였다. 남자들은 산에 올라 경작과 수렵을 하고 좀처럼 돌아오지 않았으며 질병과 천재지변도 늘 사람들의 생명을 빼앗아갔다. 장족부녀들이 애도를 표현하고 슬픔을 완화하며 재난을 피하고 이상을 토로하기 위해 장기적인 생산생활속에서 점차 장족 72 무조음악이 형성되었다.

凌云壮族的七十二巫调音乐以单人独立演唱为主，最初只有几个音阶，唱法简单，唱词多以壮话叙述为主，寄托哀思和祈祷。在不断的融合发展中，七十二巫调音乐变得越来越复杂动听，终于形成七十二调，并用凌云七十二个人文和自然景点的名称命名，这七十二景点名称都是以汉字记录的壮语地名，是当地著名的七十二"巫"（神灵）。七十二巫调是女巫师在进行巫术活动时所唱的曲调，主要是在巫婆做法事时演唱，各调有的优美柔和，有的激愤昂扬，有的悲切痛心。

The Zhuang Witch Songs with Seventy-two Tunes in Lingyun is mainly composed of solo singing, with only a few musical scales at the beginning. The singing method is simple, and the lyrics are mainly narrated in Zhuang dialect, expressing sorrow and prayer. In the process of continuous integration and development, the Zhuang Witch Songs with Seventy-two Tunes became more and more complex and pleasant, and finally formed 72 Tunes, which were named after 72 cultural and natural scenic spots in Lingyun. The names of these 72 scenic spots were all in Zhuang dialect recorded in Chinese characters, which were the local famous 72 witches (the witch god). The Zhuang Witch Songs with Seventy-two Tunes are the tunes that witches sing when they are conducting witchcraft activities and rites. Some of the tunes are beautiful and gentle, some are angry, some are sad.

릉운광족의 72 무조음악은 독자적으로 노래하는 것을 위주로 하였는데 최초에는 몇개 음계만 있었고 창법이 간단하였으며 대부분 장화로 서술하여 애도와 기도를 표시하였다. 72 무조의 끊임없는 융합과 발전 속에서 음악은 점점 더 복잡하고 감동적이 되어 마침내 72조가 형성되었으며, 일흔 두 곳의 인문 및 자연 경치의 명칭으로 명명되었다. 이 72명소의 명칭은 모두 한자로 기록된 장어 지명으로, 그 지역에서 유명한 72 무(신)이다. 72 무조는 여무당이 무술활동을 할 때 부르는 가락으로 주로 무당이 굿을 할 때 부르는데 각각 아름답고 부드러운 곡조, 격분된 곡조, 비통한 곡조가 있다.

七十二巫调音乐器具主要有两大类，静物器和响物器。静物器具有绒扇、麒麟、凤凰、香包，响物器具有铃铛、铜珠、荄。演唱时以铃声和脚踏声为主要配乐，左手拿一把铜铃扇子，右手拿一张配有铜铃的红手帕，歌声、铃声、脚踏声同起同落。在转调时不断体现出不同风格和个性，柔、凶、散板鲜明，尤其是柔板像清流的溪水又像慢飘的云雾，体现着大自然的美妙灵动。

There are two main types of witchcraft instruments: silent objects including velvet fan, kylin, phoenix, and sachets and instruments such as bell, copper beads, and hay. The main soundtrack is the sound of bells and foot during singing. A brass bell fan is hold in the left hand and a red handkerchief with a brass bell in the right hand. The sound of singing, bells and feet rising and falling are played together. While turning tones, it ceaselessly presents different styles and individual character with distinct softness, fierceness and the irregular free beat (Sanban), to reflect the beauty of nature, especially Rouban (a kind of Chinese musical terms) as soft as the clear brook and the cloud slowly drifting.

72 무조악기에는 주로 정물기와 음물기 두 가지가 있다. 정물기구로는 융부채 · 기린 · 봉황 · 향포가 있고, 향물기구로는 방울 · 구슬 · 꼴이 있다. 노래할 때는 벨소리와 발걸음 소리를 주요 음악으로 하며, 왼손에는 구리방울 부채를 들고 오른손에는 구리방울이 딸린 붉은 손수건을 들고, 노랫소리, 방울소리, 발걸음 소리를 함께 일으키고 함께 떨어진다. 곡조를 바꿀 때 서로 다른 풍격과 개성을 끊임없이 나타내며 부드럽고, 흉악하고, 산판이 선명하다. 특히 부드러운 판은 맑은 시냇물 같기도 하고, 느리게 떠가는 구름과 안개같기도 하여 대자연의 미묘한 움직임을 구현한다.

七十二巫调目前宗教功能在减弱，而更多的是被作为一种民族民间音乐被保护与留存，在丰富中国民族民间音乐种类和体裁的同时也为壮族文化的研究提供了重要的历史依据。

At present, since the religious function of Zhuang witch songs with seventy-two tunes is weakening, it is more protected and preserved as a kind of ethnic folk music, which not only enriches the types and genres of Chinese ethnic folk music, but also provides an important historical basis for the study of Zhuang culture.

72 무조는 현재 종교의 기능이 약화되고 민족민간음악으로 더욱 보호되고 보존되어 중국민족민간음악의 종류와 장르를 풍부히 하는 동시에 쫭족 문화를 연구하는데 중요한 역사적 근거를 제공하고 있다.

33. 广西文场

Guangxi Wenchang

[入选时间：2008　Time: 2008

遗产名录：第二批国家级非物质文化遗产扩展项目名录

Heritage Category: List of the second batch of National Intangible Cultural Heritage.

地域：桂林　Region: Guilin]

广西文场简称文场，又名"文玩子""小曲"等，是流行于广西桂北官话地区的汉族清唱艺术，也是广西最有代表性的传统曲艺之一，在桂林、柳州等地最为盛行。

Wenchang is short for Guangxi Wenchang, also known as "Wenwanzi" and "Xiaoqu", which is the traditional Han accapella art popular in the northern Guangxi Mandarin area, especially in Guilin and Liuzhou. It is also one of the most representative traditional folk art forms in Guangxi.

광시문장은 '文場'으로 약칭하며, '文完쯔 (문완자)', '小曲 (소곡)' 등으로도 불린다. 이는 광시성 구이베이 (桂北) 관변 지역에서 유행된 한족 청창 예술이며, 또한 광시의 가장 대표적인 전통 설창 예술의 하나이기도 하며, 계림 (桂林), 류저우 (柳州) 등 지역에서 가장 성행한다.

文场自清中后期形成至今己有两百多年历史，清代道光年间，江苏、浙江一带的时调小曲传入广西，在流传中逐渐与桂林方言融合，并受当地民歌、戏曲的影响，经历了在唱腔、曲牌、伴奏、艺术形式等方面的一系列本土化、个性化发展，至清末逐渐形成了以桂林方言演唱的、具有桂北地方特色的广西文场。

Wenchang has a history of more than 200 years since it was

formed in the middle and late Qing Dynasty. During the period of Emperor Daoguang in Qing Dynasty, the current popular tunes in Jiangsu and Zhejiang were introduced to Guangxi, which was gradually merged with Guilin dialect in the process of circulation, and influenced by local folk songs and operas. Through a series of localized and individualized development in singing, musical tunes, accompaniment and art forms, by the end of the Qing Dynasty, Guangxi Wenchang with Guilin dialect singing and local characteristics of northern Guangxi was gradually formed.

문 극 청 중후반 형성부터 지금까지 이미 200여 년 역사를 가지고 있으며 청조 때도 광년 간, 강소, 절강 일대의 시조 소곡 전래 광서, 돌에서 계림 방언과 융합하고 현지의 민요, 희곡의 영향을 겪은 곡조, 곡조 반주 예술 형식 등 방면에서 일련의 현지화, 개성 발전 청나라 말기에 이르러 점차 계림 방언으로 노래하는 구이베이 지방의 특색을 지닌 광시 문장이 형성되었다.

广西文场以唱为主，间有说白。演唱形式为数人坐唱，有生、旦、净、丑等行当之分，根据唱本中的人物来决定演唱人数，每人承担一个角色。每个演唱者还要兼操一件伴奏乐器，主奏乐器为扬琴，另有琵琶、三弦、二胡、笛子、云板、碟子等。也有化妆、穿戏装演唱的，叫"文场挂衣"。二十世纪五六十年代以后，随着文场进入剧场走上舞台，表演形式出现了"站唱"，即演唱者一人手执云板或碟子击节演唱，还出现了配以小乐队伴奏和有歌唱和舞蹈相结合的"走唱"。

Guangxi Wenchang focuses on singing, sometimes speaking, with a couple of performers sitting to sing. The roles of the performers can be divided into Sheng, Dan, Jing, Mo and Chou, and the number of performers is determined according to the characters in the singing lyrics. Each performer not only plays a role but also plays an accompaniment instrument. The main instrument is the dulcimer, and there are also pipa, three strings, erhu, flute, cloud board, dishes and so on. There are also singing with makeup and costumes, which is called "Wenchang with costumes". After the 1950s and 1960s, as Wenchang was played on the theatre stage, standing singing form appeared, in which singers singing while holding a cloud board and beating dishes. Later, Walking singing form accompanied by a small band and the combination of singing and dancing also came into being.

광서문장에서는 노래를 위주로 하고 중간에 대사 (대사와 대사)도 있다. 공연형식은 여러 사람이 앉아서 노래하며, 생, 단, 정, 추 등 행별로 구분되며, 대본 속의 인물에 따라 공연하는 인원수를 결정하고, 각자가 한 배역을 맡는다. 창자마다 반주악기도 하나 연주해야 하는데 주주악기는 양금이고 또 비파, 삼현, 얼후, 피리, 운판, 접시 등이 있다. 또 화장을 하거나 전통의상을 입고 공연하는 사람도 있는데, 이를 '文마당걸이 (文마당걸이)'라고 한다. 1950, 60년대 이후 문장이 극장 무대에 오르면서 공연형식인 '역창', 즉 한 사람이 운판이나 접시를 들고 격절하는 '역창'이

등장했고, 작은 악대 반주에 노래와 춤이 어우러진 '걸창'도 등장했다.

广西文场的传统唱词丰富, 所唱曲目内容多取自明清的传奇小说。成套的唱本有《玉簪记》、《白蛇传》、《琵琶记》、《西厢记》、《红楼梦》等作品, 加上单出唱本《双下山》、《王婆骂鸡》、《东方朔上寿》等60出左右。段子有《武二探兄》、《醉打山门》、《贵妃醉酒》等近100个。近年来创作了一些歌颂桂林山水风光的抒情小段, 如《画中游》、《仙境怎比我桂林》、《七星夜游》等。

The traditional singing lyrics of Guangxi Wenchang is rich, most of which are taken from the legend stories of Ming and Qing Dynasties: in terms of lyric sets, there are "Story of Jade Hairpin", "Tale of White Snake", "Story of Pipa", Romance of the Western Chamber", and "Dream of Red Mansions"; in terms of single singing lyric, there are about 60 pieces, including "Shuangxiashan"," Old Woman Wang scold chicken" and "Dongfangshuo celebrating birthday"; in terms of episode, there are about 100 pieces, such as "WuEr visiting his elder brother", "Beating the gate after drinking" and "Drunken beauty". Recently some new lyrics about the beautiful mountain and water scenery of Guilin are created, such as "Travle in the pictures", "fairyland is no better than Guilin", and "Night travel around Seven Star Mountain".

광서문장에는 전통가사가 풍부하며 노래곡목의 내용은 대부분 명청시기의 전기소설에서 가져왔다. 완결판본으로는 「옥잠기」, 「백사면」, 「비파전」, 「서상기」, 「홍루몽」 등이 있고, 단발판으로는 「쌍하산」, 「왕파가 닭을 욕하다」, 「동방삭상수」 등 약 60편이 있다. 단자는 「무이탐형」, 「취타산문」, 「귀비의 취중」 등 100개에 달한다. 최근에 「그림 중류(中流)」, 「선경(仙境)은 어찌 계림(桂林)에 비할 수 있는가」, 「칠성의 밤여행(七星夜行)」 등과 같이 계림의 산수와 풍경을 노래하는 서정적인 소단을 창작하였다.

文场演唱者把文场唱词、音乐之美融入唱腔，把唱词中的情感和音乐的韵律之美用唱腔艺术表现出来，形成文场的艺术之美。如今，广西文场伴随着美丽的桂林山水，以其传统的艺术魅力，以新的内容和新的表现手段，展现在文艺舞台上，是广西珍贵的非物质文化遗产。

Singers of Wenchang incorporate the beauty of music and lyrics into their singing styles, and express the emotion and the beauty of music rhythm with their singing art, forming the artistic beauty of Wenchang. Nowadays, along with the beautiful Guilin landscape, Guangxi Wenchang has been presented to the art stage by means of its traditional artistic magic, new content and new performing skills, which is a valuable Intangible Cultural Heritage of Guangxi.

문장가창자는 문장가사와 음악의 미를 곡조에 융합시켜 가사의 감정과 음악의 운률미를 곡조예술로 표현함으로써 문장의 예술미를 형성한다. 현재 광서문화 공연장은 아름다운 계림의 산수와 함께 그 전통적인 예술매력과 새로운 내용, 새로운 표현수단으로 문예무대에 소개되고 있는 광서의 귀중한 무형문화유산이다.

34. 桂林渔鼓

Guilin Yugu Tunes

[入选时间：2014 Time: 2014

遗产名录：第四批国家级非物质文化遗产名录

Heritage Category: List of the fourth batch of National Intangible Cultural Heritage.

地域：桂林 Region: Guilin]

桂林渔鼓俗称道情，又名广西渔鼓，是桂林市的地方传统说唱艺术。桂林渔鼓吸取了湖北道情、祁阳渔鼓、全州渔鼓的音乐元素，又独具自身风格，曲目的内容有厚重的文化底蕴，丰富了广西曲艺历史、民间艺术史和音乐史。同时，桂林渔鼓作为珠江流域、长江流域民间曲艺的结晶，记录和印证着中原文化、楚文化与骆越文化之间的相互传播、撞击和交融的历史。

Yugu (literally fishing drum) is a percussion instrument made of bamboo. A Yugu performance is a chant of folk tales to the accompaniment of such an instrument. Guilin Yugu is generally called Daoqing (a form of folk art), also known as Guangxi Yugu, is a traditional local chanting art of Guilin. Even though it absorbed the musical elements from Hubei Daoqing, Qiyang Yugu and Quanzhou Yugu, it also kept its own style, with the contents of songs rich in cultural deposits, enriching the history of Guangxi Quyi, folk art and music. Meanwhile as the folk art quintessence of the Pearl River Basin and the Yangtze River Basin, Guilin Yugu records and witnesses the history of Cultural transmission, collision and integration among Central Culture, Chu Culture and Luoyue Culture.

계림어고(桂林漁鼓)는 속칭 도정(道情)이라고도 하며 광서어고(广西)라고도 하는데 계림시의 지방 전통 설창예술이다. 계림(桂林) 어고는 호북(湖北) 도정(道情), 치양(治陽) 어고(漁鼓), 전주(전주) 어고의 음악요소를 흡수하여 독자적인 풍격을 갖추었으며, 곡목의 내용은 두터운 문화내력을 가지고 있고 광시 (廣西)의 설창예술사, 민간 예술사와 음악사를 풍부하게 하였다. 또한, 계림 어고는 주장 강 유역과 창장 강 유역의 민간 설창 예술의 결정체로서, 중원 문화, 초나라 문화, 낙월 문화 사이의 상호 전파와 충돌, 융합의 역사를 기록하고 증명하고 있다.

桂林渔鼓的起源, 一种说法是, 宋代时由北方传入桂林, 受桂林方言、音乐的影响而形成;另一种说法是, 明末清初、民国期间湖南的渔鼓艺人在桂林传唱渔鼓并落户桂林, 开了桂林渔鼓的先河。此后, 桂林的市井坊间乡村瑶寨都有渔鼓的鼓声荡漾。即使按后一种说法, 桂林渔鼓也有400年历史之久。

About the origin of Guilin Yugu, one story told that it was introduced to Guilin from the north in Song Dynasty and formed under the influence of Guilin dialect and music. Another story put it in the way that the chanting performance form of Guilin Yugu had been greatly influenced by Hunan Yugu, of which the artists started to settle in Guilin and spread Yugu tunes as the pioneers of Guilin Yugu during periods of late Ming Dynasty, Early Qing Dynasty and the Republic of China. Since then Yugu tunes were heard among the streets, villages and Yao group inhabited regions of Guilin. According to this story, Guilin Yugu has a history of 400 years.

계림 어고의 기원에 대해 일설로는 송조때 북방에서 계림에 전해져 계림 방언과 음악의 영향을 받아 형성되었다고 한다. 다른 일설로는 명말, 청초, 민국 시기에 후난의 어고 예술인들이 계림에서 어고를 부르고 정착시켜 계림 어고의 효시로 삼았다는 설이 있다. 그후 계림의 시정과 농촌의 요민마을에는 모두 어고의 북소리가 울려 퍼졌다. 후자의 견해에 따르더라도 계림어고는 400년의 역사를 갖고 있다.

在20世纪30年代, 当时负有盛名的桂林盲艺人王仁和向已落户桂林的原湖南祁阳渔鼓艺人和桂林兴安渔鼓艺人学习渔鼓,在掌握了渔鼓的基本曲式唱腔的基础又上发 挥自身艺术素养形成了 具有浓郁地方特色的渔鼓说唱艺术风格。他在继承渔鼓音乐的基础上吸收当地民间艺术的元素,经过多年探索又创造了南 北路板式变化体, 北路表现 明朗、欢快、高亢、激昂的情绪, 南路 则表现忧郁、低沉、思索、 悲愤之情。

In 1930s, Wang Renhe, the current renowned blind artist, learnt Yugu from Qiyang Yugu artists of Hunan, who had settled in Guilin, and the elder Xing'an Yugu artists of Guilin. By exerting his artistic capacity he fully explored the potential of this art on the basis of the basic form and singing of Yugu, and formed the chanting style of Yugu with strong local characteristics. After many years of exploration and inheritance of Yugu, he also created a board variant of South and North style by absorbing the local folk art, among which the North Style is full of bright, joyful and passionate feelings, while the South Style is grave, low, grief and angry.

20세기 30년대에 유명한 계림맹인 왕인화는 이미 계림에 정착한 원호남성 기양어고예인과 계림 흥안어고예인에게서 어고를 배우고 어고의 기본식창조를 장악한 기초우에서 자신의 예술소양을 발휘하여 지방특색이 짙은 어고설창 예술풍격을 형성하였다. 그는 어고음악을 계승하는 기초에서 현지 민간예술의 요소를 흡수하여 다년간의 탐색을 거쳐 또 남북도로 형식의 변화체를 창조하였는데 북로는 명랑하고 명랑하며 우렁차고 격앙된 정서를 나타내고 남로는 우울하고 나지막하며 사색적이고 비분의 감정을 나타낸다.

桂林渔鼓伴奏的主要乐器是渔鼓, 渔鼓是由直径约十一公分长约二尺的楠竹制成, 鼓面可蒙上蛇皮、蛙皮或猪板油皮, 另配以简板、二胡、中胡、月琴、中阮、三弦、笛子、碟子、酒杯等。演唱形式有两种, 一是"打单筒", 即一人左手抱渔鼓, 右手击鼓, 自打自唱; 第二种是带伴奏、伴唱形式, 有二人组、三人组、五至七八人甚至十余人不等的组合。

The major accompaniment instrument to the performance is Yugu, which is made of bamboo, 11 centimeters in diameter and 2 feet in length, and snake skin, frog skin and pig skin covered on top of it. It is also matched by plate, erhu, zhonghu, yueqi, zhongruan, three-stringed plucked instrument, flutes, saucers and wine cups. There are two kinds of singing forms: one is solo performance, in which one player sings and play the instruments at the same time, with the left hand holding Yugu and right hand beating the drum; the other is accompaniment performance, in which groups vary in number of two, three, five to eight and even more than ten.

계림어고 반주의 주요 악기는 어고(漁鼓)이다. 어고는 지름 약 1cm에 길이 약 2자(尺)인 녹대(南竹)로 만들어지고, 북 위에 뱀가죽, 개구리가죽 혹은 돼지기름 껍질을 씌울 수 있으며, 또 간판(간판), 얼후(二胡), 중호(中湖), 월금(月金), 중원(中元), 삼현(三縣), 피리, 접시, 술잔 등을 붙여 만든다. 노래 형식은 두 가지다. 하나는 '외통치기', 즉 한 사람이 왼손으로 어고를 잡고 오른손으로 북을 치면서 스스로 노래하는 것이다. 두 번째 종류는 반주·반창 형식으로 2인조, 3인조, 5~7~8명 심지어는 10여 명으로 구성된 그룹도 있다.

桂林渔鼓的代表性传统曲目有《玉带记》、《蓝丝带》、《薛家将故事》、《白蛇传》、《三姑记》等。反映现代生活的曲目有《二姐做梦》、《水上抓匪》、《五分钱》、《心红志壮》、《王老头学文化》等。

The traditional representative repertories of Yugu include *Tales of Jade Belt, Blue Ribbon, Story of Xue Family, Legend of the White Snake, and Tales of Sangu* and so on. The current repertories showing modern life include The *Dream of the Second Elder Sister, Catching Bandits on Water, Five Cents, Ambitious Heart, Elder Man Wang Learning*, etc..

계림어고의 대표적인 전통곡목은 '옥대기', '푸른 리본', '설가장이야기', '백사전', '삼고기' 등이다. 현대생활을 반영한 곡목으로는 「둘째 누나의 꿈」, 「수상에서 비적을 잡다」, 「오전」, 「심홍지장」, 「왕영감이 문화를 배우다」 등이 있다.

桂林渔鼓是桂林传统文化的重要表现形式, 是多地域文化融合的"活化石", 从其中折射出古代社会生活的人生百态, 对研究广西的生活史、曲艺史等很有借鉴意义。

Guilin Yugu is an important representation of Guilin Culture, and a living fossil of cultural integration. The various forms of ancient life reflected in it provide a significant value for the study of the life history and Quyi history of Guangxi.

계림어고는 계림 전통문화의 중요한 표현형식이며, 다지역 문화가 융합된 '살아있는 화석'으로 그중에서 고대사회생활의 백태를 반영하여 광시(广西)의 생활사, 설창예술사 등을 연구하는데 큰 참고가 있다.

35. 侗族木构建筑营造技艺

Architectural craftsmanship for timber-framed structures of Dong Ethnic Group

[入选时间：2006   Time: 2006

遗产名录：第一批国家级非物质文化遗产名录
Heritage Category: List of the first batch of National Intangible Cultural Heritage.

地域：柳州   Region: Liuzhou]

侗族木构建筑营造技艺流传于广西三江侗族自治县。这种建筑技艺始于魏唐的干栏式建筑，已有一千多年的历史。侗族木构建筑种类繁多，主要有民居（木楼）、鼓楼、风雨桥、寨门、井亭、凉亭等。侗族木构建筑依山傍水，式样美观，技艺精巧，体现了侗族工匠们高超的建筑工艺水平和精神寄托。

The architectural craftsmanship for timber-framed structures of Dong ethnic group spread in Dong Autonomous County of Sanjiang in Guangxi. This architecture technique originated from the stilt-style architecture in Wei and Tang dynasties, which has a history of more than one thousand years. Dong timber-framed building has a wide range, including residential houses (wooden building), drum tower, wind and rain bridges, village gates, well pavilions and pavilions. Being built near rivers and mountains, beautiful in style and exquisite in craftsmanship, Dong timber-framed building reflects the excellent construction technique and spiritual sustenance of craftsman of Dong ethnic group.

동족의 목구조건축기예는 광시싼장동족자치현에 널리 전해지고 있다. 이런 건축기예는 위당시기의 간란식건축에서 시작되었는데 이미 1,000여년의 역사를 갖고있다. 동족 목조 건축물은 종류가 매우 많은데 주로 민가(목조), 고루, 풍우교, 촌문, 정자, 량정 등이 있다. 동족 목조건축은 산과

물을 끼고 모양이 아름답고 기예가 정교하여 동족 장인들의 높은 건축공예수준과 정신적기양을 보여준다.

鼓楼、风雨桥、凉亭被并称为"侗族建筑三宝"。传统侗族建村、建寨之前需要首先建成鼓楼。鼓楼是召集村民集会、议事的场所；风雨桥主要是解决侗族人民依山跨水的交通问题，成为侗族村寨村民聚居的重要活动场，一般建于村口或村尾，成为村寨的门户，有着为侗族村寨祈福禳灾的作用；凉亭在侗族文化中也有聚会功能。

Drum Tower, wind and rain Bridge and pavilion are the "Three treasures of Dong architecture". Drum towers are built before building villages according to traditional Dong culture and it is a place for villagers to gather and discuss village events; Wind and rain bridges are built to solve the traffic problems of Dong people who live by the water and mountains, and they are usually built at the entrance or end of the village and served as the gateway of the village as well as an important gathering place for Dong villagers. Wind and rain bridges also have the function of discarding disasters and praying for good luck in Dong villages. The pavilions are also the places for gathering in Dong culture.

고루(鼓樓)·풍우교(風雨橋)·량정(凉亭)은 '동족 건축 3보(三寶)'로 함께 불린다. 전통 동족은 마을과 마을을 건설하기 전에 먼저 고루를 지어야 한다. 고루는 마을 사람들을 소집하여 집회를 열고 의사를 토의하는 장소이다. 비바람다리는 주로 동족이 산에 의지하고 물을 건너가는 교통문제를 해결하며 동족 마을에서 중요한 활동장이 된다. 일반적으로 마을 입구나 마을 끝에 건설하여 마을의 문호로서 동족 마을의 복을 빌고 재앙을 떨쳐버리는 역할을 한다. 동족 문화에서 정자는 모임 기능을 하기도 한다.

侗族民间工匠建筑才能的高超体现在建造时不用绘制图纸和模型, 整体构思全在脑海中, 仅凭简单的竹签为标尺, 靠独特的设计标注, 使用普通的木匠工具和木料就能制造出样式各异、造型美观的楼桥, 设计之精巧, 造型之美观, 均令人叹为观止。

Dong folk craftsmen have superb architectural talent, and they do not need drawings and models when constructing buildings, bridges and residential buildings. The blueprint is in their minds, and they could produce buildings and bridges with different styles and appealing appearances by using bamboo sticks as rulers, relying on the unique design and mark, and using ordinary carpenter tools and wood materials. The exquisite design and beautiful appearance are breathtaking.

동족 민간 건축 장인들의 뛰어난 구현할 수 있는지을 때 제작 도면과 모형을 쓰지 않고 전체적인 구상 전 머릿속에서 간단 한 꼬치 만으로 잣대로 독특 한 디자인으로 표시 된 보통의 목수 도구와 목재를 만들면 양식이 서로 다른 다리, 긴 층 설계의 정교, 조형의 아름 다우나, 모두 감탄했다.

侗族木构建筑技艺的另一大特色是：凿榫打眼、穿梁接拱、立柱连枋不用一颗铁钉，全以榫卯连接，结构牢固，接合缜密，有极高的工艺和艺术价值。楼、桥上的各种图案及雕梁画栋寄托了侗族人民祈望风调雨顺、五谷丰登的美好愿望和美学追求，是侗族文化特性的集中体现。

Another unique feature of Dong architectural craftsmanship is that the whole building of the Dong timber-framed works is drilled with mortises, and the brackets, upright columns and cross beams are connected by mortise and tenon without a single iron nail. The structure is sturdy and meticulous with high craft and artistic value. The various patterns, beam carvings and paintings on the buildings and bridges embody Dong people's wish for good weather, abundant grain and aesthetic pursuit, which are the epitomization of Dong culture.

동족 목조 건축기술은 또 다른 특색이 있는데, 장부를 파고 들보를 꿰어

아치를 연결하고, 기둥을 세워 목조와 목부를 연결하며, 구조가 튼튼하고 접합력이 세어 공예와 예술적 가치가 높다. 누각과 다리의 각종 도안과 조각한 기둥과 그림은 동족의 아름다운 소망과 미학적 추구를 담고 있으며 동족문화 특성의 집중적인 구현이다.

36. 壮族织锦技艺

Craftsmanship of Zhuang Brocade

[入选时间：2006   Time: 2006

遗产名录：第一批国家级非物质文化遗产名录

Heritage Category: List of the first batch of National Intangible Cultural Heritage.

地域： 百色   Region: Baise]

锦是具有多种彩色花纹的丝织品。在中国古代丝织品中，"锦"的生产工艺要求最高、织造难度最大。它用彩色丝线织出优美的花纹，材料考究，制作费工，因而也是古代最贵重的织物。

Brocade is a kind of silk fabric with various color patterns. Among the silk fabrics in ancient China, brocade is the most difficult one to produce and requires the top manufacturing technique. With beautiful patterns made of colored silk threads, brocade is also the most valuable fabric in ancient times for its exquisite materials and sophisticated making technique.

비단은 여러 가지 채색 무늬를 가진 견직물이다. 중국 고대 견직물 중 '비단'의 생산 공예 요구가 가장 높고 직조하는 난이도가 가장 크다. 채색견사를 이용하여 아름다운 무늬를 짜내는데 재료가 아름답고 제작품이 많이 들어 고대에 가장 귀중한 직물이였다.

壮锦与成都的蜀锦、苏州的宋锦、南京的云锦并称"中国四大名锦"。壮锦利用棉线或丝线编织而成，以结实耐用、技艺精巧、图案别致、花纹精美著称，其热烈、开朗的民族格调体现了壮族人民对美好生活的追求和向往。

Zhuang brocade, together with Sichuan brocade in Chengdu,

Song brocade in Suzhou and Yunjin brocade in Nanjing, is known as "the four famous brocade of China". Zhuang brocade is woven from cotton and silk thread. It is famous for its durability, superb craftsmanship, unique design and exquisite decorative patterns. The warm and cheerful national style in it reflected Zhuang people's pursuit and yearn for better life.

장금은 청두의 촉금, 쑤저우의 송금, 난징의 원금과 함께 중국 4대 명금으로 불린다. 면사나 견사로 짠 웅장한 비단은 튼튼하고 내구성이 있으며, 기교가 정교하고, 도안이 독특하고, 문양이 정교하여 유명하며, 그 열정적이고 명랑한 민족 풍격은 아름다운 생활에 대한 좡족 국민들의 추구와 동경을 보여준다.

壮锦作为工艺美术织品,是壮族人民最精彩的文化创造之一,其历史也非常悠久。据古籍文献记载,真正能够称为"壮锦"的纺织品出现于宋代,距今已有九百多年。这一时期,壮族的纺织业进一步发展,除普通的布帛以外,还出现了丝、麻、丝棉交织的锦。宋代"白质方纹,佳丽厚重"的布,就是早期的壮锦。明清时期,壮锦已发展到用多种色彩的绒线编织,使壮锦呈现出绚丽的色彩,虽仍为皇室贡品,但平民百姓亦可享用。清末民初,壮锦开始衰落。历经千余年发展壮锦经历了从单色到五彩斑斓,图案花纹从简单到繁复的发展变化,现在的壮锦有自成体系的三大种类、20多个品种和50多种图案。

Zhuang brocade, as an arts and crafts fabric, is one of the most splendid cultural creations of Zhuang people with long history. According to the records of ancient documents, the textile can be called "Zhuang brocade" appeared in Song Dynasty over 900 years ago. During this period, the textile industry of the Zhuang group received further development. In addition to plain cloth, there was also the appearance of brocade interwoven with silk and cloth, hemp and silk floss. In Song Dynasty, the beautiful and heavy cloth with white square patterns was regarded as the early Zhuang brocade. During Ming and Qing Dynasties, Zhuang brocade had been woven with various colors of wool, which left Zhuang brocade with gorgeous colors. Although it was a tribute to the royal family, it could also be used by civilians. In late Qing Dynasty and early Republic of China, Zhuang brocade began to decline. After more than one thousand years of development, in terms of color, Zhuang brocade has experienced from monochrome to multi-color, and in pattern, it has been changed from being simple to being complicated. Now Zhuang brocade has formed its own system of 3 types, over 20 varieties and more than 50 patterns.

공예미술직물로서 좡족인민의 가장 다채로운 문화창조의 하나로서 그 역사가 아주 유구하다. 고서 문헌의 기록에 따르면 정말 '웅장한 금색'이라고 부를 수 있는 방직품은 지금으로부터 900여 년 전에 송대에 출현했다고 한다. 이 시기 쫭족의 방직업은 진일보 발전하여 일반 부직물 외에도 견사, 삼, 견직물을 교직한 비단도 나타났다. 송조때의 "백색의 네모난 무늬가 아름답고 중후한 "천이 바로 초기의 장금이다. 명청시기에 이르러 장금은 이미 여러가지 색깔의 털실로 짜여져 화려한 색채를 띠게 되였으며 황실의 공물로 사용되었지만 평민들도 사용할 수 있었다. 청조말기와 민국초기에 장금은 쇠락하기 시작하였다. 1,000여 년의 발전을 거쳐 드넓은 비단은 단색에서 오색찬란함으로, 간단한 패턴에서 복잡한 패턴까지 발전과 변화를 겪었으며, 현재 드넓은 비단은 3가지 체계, 20여 종의 품종과 50여 종의 도안이 있다.

壮锦的编织技艺一般需要借助装有支撑系统、传动装置、分综装置和提花装置的手工织机，机上设有"花笼"用以提织花纹图案，用花笼起花为壮锦织机的最大特点。壮锦用麻线或棉线染色，以棉纱为经，以各种彩色丝绒为纬，在织机上用通经断纬的方法进行手工编织。

The weaving technique of Zhuang brocade usually requires the aid of handlooms equipped with supporting system, transmission, separation and jacquard devices. The "flower cage" on the loom is used to weave patterns, which is the most prominent feature of Zhuang brocade loom. Zhuang brocade is dyed with hemp and cotton thread, using cotton yarn as warp and various color velvet as weft, and the weaving technique is called "the warps connected and the wefts cracked".

드랍비단의 편직 기술은 일반적으로 지지 시스템, 전동 장치, 분합 장치 및 자카드 장치가 설치되어 있는 수공 직기의 도움을 필요로 하며, 기계에 꽃무늬 도안을 짜는 "꽃초롱"이 설치되어 있으며, 꽃초롱으로 꽃초롱을 짜는 것은 드랍비단직기의 가장 큰 특징이다. 붕대는 삼실 또는 면실로 염색하고 면사를 날실로 하고 여러가지 채색벨루어를 씨실로 하여 직기에 날실을 통과시키고 씨실을 끊는 방법으로 수공으로 짜낸다.

壮锦图案构成的式样大致有三种：一是平纹上织二方连续和四方连续的几何纹，组成连绵的几何图案，显得朴素而明快；二是以各种几何纹为底，上饰动植物图案，形成多层次的复合图形，图案清晰而有浮雕感；三是用多种几何纹大小结合，方圆穿插，编织成繁密而富于韵律感的复合几何图案，有严谨和谐之美。

The patterns of Zhuang brocade can be divided into three types. The first one is to weave numerous two consecutive squares and four consecutive squares patterns on the plain weave, which forms a simple and bright continuous geometric designs; the second is to use various geometric patterns as the base, decorated with animal and plant patterns to form multi-level composite graphics with clear designs and relief; the third is to use a variety of geometric patterns in different sizes and weave them into dense and rhythmic composite geometric patterns, which shows the beauty of preciseness and harmony.

웅장금도안은 대체로 3가지 양식으로 구성되었다. 첫째는 평직물우에 2방형과 4방형이 연속된 기하무늬를 짜내여 연속된 기하도안을 구성하여 소박하면서도 명쾌하게 보인다. 둘째, 각종 기하무늬를 밑그림으로 하고 그 위에 동식물도안을 장식하여 다차원의 복합도형을 형성하였는데 도안이 뚜렷하고 부각감이 있다. 셋째, 여러가지 기하무늬의 크기를 결합하고 네모와 원을 교차시켜 촘촘하고 운율감이 있는 복합기하도안을 엮어 내여 엄밀하고 조화로운 미를 갖고있다.

壮锦是壮族的优秀文化遗产之一，它不仅可为我国少数民族纺织技艺的研究提供生动的实物材料，还可以为中国乃至世界的纺织史增添活态的例证，对继承和弘扬民族文化，增强民族自尊心起到积极的作用。

Zhuang brocade is one of the excellent cultural heritage of Zhuang group. It not only provides vivid materials for the textile technology research of ethnic minorities in China, but also adds living examples to the textile history of China as well as the world. It plays a positive role in the inheritance and promotion of national culture and the enhancement of the national self-esteem.

쫭족의 우수한 문화유산의 하나인 '장금'은 중국 소수민족의 방직기예를 연구하는데 생동한 실물자료를 제공할 뿐만 아니라 중국 더 나아가서는 세계 방직사에 생생한 실례를 더해주고 민족문화를 계승하고 고양하며 민족자존심을 높이는데 적극적인 역할을 한다.

37. 钦州坭兴陶

Qinzhou Nixing pottery

[入选时间：2008　Time: 2008

遗产名录：第二批国家级非物质文化遗产名录

Heritage Category: List of the second batch of National Intangible Cultural Heritage.

地域：钦州　Region: Qinzhou]

钦州坭兴陶与壮锦技艺一同被认定为目前广西最具民族特色的二件宝，也是钦州最名著名的特产之一。钦州坭兴陶，简称坭兴陶，又名坭兴桂陶，以广西钦州市钦江东西两岸特有紫红陶土为原料，经严选细练，采东、西泥之结合，东软为肉，西硬为骨，挖取东泥、西泥后，按软六硬四混合，骨肉相互支撑得当，始方为上乘之品。将东泥、西泥按一定的比例混合后，经过湿球磨、过筛、沉淀、压滤、真空练泥等工序，备好可塑胚料，然后通过拉胚成型。

Qinzhou Nixing pottery together with Zhuang brocade is considered as the two treasures with distinct national features of Guangxi Zhuang Autonomous Region at present, and it is also one of the most famous local specialties in Qinzhou. Nixing pottery, short form of Qinzhou Nixing pottery, also known as Nixing Gui Pottery, chooses the unique purple clay in the east and west sides of Qin River in Guangxi as raw materials. The clay in the eastern bank is soft like meat while the western is hard like bone. After strict selection and refinement, the combination of the clay from the east and west banks is adopted. The best product ratio in terms of soft and hard clay is three to two. After mixing in proportion, the sculpable base is prepared through procedures of grinding, sieving, precipitation, pressure filtration, vacuum mud drilling of the wet ball, and then the shape is formed by drawing the base.

친저우니싱타오(钦州坭興陶)는 광서좡족자치구에서 장금기교와 함께 민족 특색이 있는 2대 보물로 인정되고 있으며 친저우의 가장 유명한 특산품의 하나이기도 하다. 친저우니싱타오(钦州坭興陶)는 광시 친저우시 친강 동서 양안의 특유한 자홍도토를 원료로 하며, 엄선하고 섬세하게 채취하여 동(東)과 서(西)의 진흙을 혼합하여 동(東)과 서(西)의 진흙을 채취한 후, 연(燕)과 경(經)의 4가지를 혼합하여 골육(骨肉)과 살(肉)이 서로 잘 받쳐(주)어야 상등품이다. 동니·서니·진흙을 일정한 비율로 혼합한 후 습구 제마, 체 거르기, 침전, 압려·진공의 과정을 거쳐 제조 가능한 재료를 준비한 후 배뽑기를 통해 성형한다.

钦州坭兴陶最大的特点是不施釉而采用雕刻进行装饰。装饰艺术上采用雕、刻、剔的技法，在泥坯上雕、刻、剔出花卉、人物、山水等图案，并可填入白、赭等色泥抹平。坭兴陶因用料内含丰富三氧化二铁成份，经烧成还原成氧化铁、氧化亚铁显铁青色。铁青色与原料紫红色混合在一起，由于窑炉中的气氛不同，氧化还原程度不同，其显色亦产生微妙的变化，同一窑炉中的每件都不同，显得别具一格。

The most prominent feature of Qinzhou Nixing pottery is the use of sculpture for decoration instead of glazing. People engrave and scrape flowers, figures, landscapes and other patterns on the clay paste to decorate and use white and reddish-brown clay for leveling. Since Nixing pottery is rich in iron trioxide, it deoxidizes the iron oxide and ferrous oxide after sintering and turns steel blue. When the colors of steel blue and fuchsia mix in the condition of different temperatures in the furnace and the different degrees of REDOX, it also produces subtle changes in the color of each piece of the products even in the same furnace, making a unique style.

친저우니싱타오는 유약을 칠하지 않고 조각하여 장식한 것이 가장 큰 특징이다. 장식예술에서는 조각, 각, 파내는 기법을 사용하여 흙벽자에 화훼, 인물, 산수 등의 도안을 새기고 파내고, 또 흰색, 홍가 등 색깔의 진흙을 채워 평평하게 칠할 수 있다. 니싱 도자기는 원료가 풍부한 삼산화이철 성분을 포함하고 있기 때문에, 구워 산화철, 산화 아철로 환원되어 철청색을 나타낸다. 철청색과 원료인 자홍색이 한데 섞여 있는데 가마안의 분위기와 산화환원정도가 다름에 따라 그 색깔도 미묘하게 변화되는데 같은 가마안의 건물마다 서로 달라 독특한 풍채를 띤다.

同时，泥兴陶的"窑变"艺术在国内陶瓷行业中绝无仅有，艺术品位极高，故有"中国一绝"之称。即当炉盘上钦州坭兴陶升到1200度的临界点时，偶然有极少量的坯体在原来铁红色的基础上隐约呈现出古铜、紫红、铁青、金黄、墨绿等多种色泽，以及天斑、虎纹等纹路变化。经高温烧成后，打磨掉表层氧化物，加以精工琢磨光滑，形成所谓"白器红花"或"红器白花"，甚为雅致。

The art of "furnace transformation" of Nixing pottery is of high artistic taste in domestic ceramic industry, and could be called "a unique one in China". When Qinzhou Nixing pottery on the furnace plate was burned to the critical point of 1200 degrees, occasionally a very small amount of the paste turned to a variety of colors from originally rust to vaguely bronze, purple, steel blue, gold and dark green, and leaving the patterns such as the sky spots and tiger stripes. After being burned at high temperature, the surface oxide on the pottery is polished until glossy and forms the so-called elegant products of "white pottery with red flower" or "red pottery with white flower".

또한 니흥도의 "요변"예술은 국내 도자기업계에서 유일무이하며 예술 품위가 아주 높아 "중국에서 제일가는 작품"이라고 불린다. 즉, 난로 위의 친저우니싱타오가 1200도의 경계점에 이르렀을 때 우연히 소량의 벽체가 원래의 철홍색 바탕 위에 구리, 자흥, 철청, 금황, 검푸른 등 다양한 색상과 하늘의 반점, 호랑이무늬 등의 무늬의 변화를 나타나게 된다. 고온을 거쳐, 표면의 산화물을 닦아 내고, 정제하고 다듬어 매끈하게 하여, 소위 "백기홍화" 또는 "홍기백화"가 형성되며, 매우 우아하다.

钦州制陶人不断发扬传承桂陶的制陶精髓，将"双料混炼、自然素面、窑变出彩、陶刻创作、陶艺造型"五项传统制陶工艺淋漓尽致地运用于陶器艺术创作中，独特地运用钦江两岸的红泥白泥烧制出古朴、典雅、厚重的坭兴陶，在钦州千年的历史发展长河中创造了千年传奇的人间奇迹。特别是进入清朝咸丰年以后，坭兴陶在承载千年传奇等深厚文化基础上化蛹成蝶，开创了艺术升华的新篇章。1915年在美国巴拿马国际博览会获得金奖，成为中国四大名陶之一。

Qinzhou pottery craftsmen continuously improve and inherit the ceramics essence of Gui pottery. Five traditional pottery artistry to produce visual and artistic effects in pottery making, namely "the mixed tempering of two kinds of clay, naturally tempering without glaze and colors, changing colors in the furnace, creation by means of engraving and printing, and pottery modelling", are adopted and the clays in the two sides of the Qin River are used to make the simple, elegant, and massive Nixing pottery, which has created the human miracle of the legend in the history of Qinzhou for thousands of years. Especially after the period of Emperor Xianfeng in Qing Dynasty Nixing pottery entered a new phase of artistic sublimation on its thousand-year culture basis. In 1915, it won the gold medal in Panama International Exposition and became one of the four famous ceramics in China.

친저우 (钦州)의 도자기 제조인들은 끊임없이 계도기의 정수를 발전시켜

'2가지 재료의 혼합, 자연 소면, 가마 변신 채색, 도기 조각 창작, 도기 조형' 등 5가지 전통 도기 제조 공예를 철저하게 도기 예술 창작에 응용하였으며, 독특하게 친강 양안의 붉은 진흙과 흰 진흙을 이용하여 고풍스럽고 우아하며 중후한 니싱 도기를 구워 냈다. 친져우는 천년의 역사발전속에서 천년의 전기적인 인간기적을 창조하였다. 특히 청조 함풍년에 들어선 후 니흥도는 천년의 전기를 담는 등 깊은 문화적 토대에서 번데기로 변하여 나비가 됨으로써 예술적승화의 새로운 장을 열어놓았다. 1915년에는 미국의 파나마국제박람회에서 금상을 수상하여 중국 4대 명도자기의 하나로 되였다.

参考文献

[1]　李斯颖. 布洛陀：壮族创世史诗[M]. 广西教育出版社, 2022.

[2]　黎学锐.歌谣刘三姐[M]. 广西人民出版社, 2011.

[3]　韦其麟. 百鸟衣[M].中国青年出版社, 1956.

[4]　韦其麟.壮族民间文学概观[M]. 广西人民出版社, 1988.

[5]　邓宇航.口头传统的沿袭：富川瑶族民歌的传播学研究—以平地瑶"蝴蝶歌"为例[J].广西民族研究,2020(01):164-170.

[6]　杜长青,刘靖南,杜科锋.广西藤县舞狮开展现状的田野考察[J].当代体育科技,2014,4(18):147-148.

[7]　狄松菊.广西非物质文化遗产桂林渔鼓的田野调查分析[J].中国民族博览,2021,No.212(16):127-128+175.

[8]　何成战,梁松,刘凯.广西传统侗族建筑数字化平台建设与研究[J].广西民族大学学报(自然科学版),2017,23(02):78-81.

[9]　黄钰,俸代瑜.瑶族传统节日文化[J].广西民族研究,1994(04):23-35.

[10]　黄小明,赖程程,胡晶莹.毛南族还愿仪式舞蹈"条套"的动作特征与文化内涵——广西环江毛南族民间舞蹈现状考察[J].艺术百家,2009,25(05):184-188.

[11]　蒋东升,唐元超,李利,范佳祥.民族传统体育历史演变路径及启示——基于国家级非物质文化遗产瑶族金锣舞的体育人类学调查[J].贵州民族研究,2019,40(10):123-127.

[12]　蓝怀昌. 布努瑶创世史诗—密洛陀[M], 中国民间文艺出版社, 1988.

[13]　蓝武芳.海洋文化的重要非物质文化遗产——京族哈节的调查报告[J].民间文化论坛,2006(03):94-99.

[14]　廖明君.瑶族盘王节[J].广西民族研究,2009(04):211+209-210.

[15]　廖明君.瑶山中的铜鼓声——图说田林瑶族铜鼓舞[J].歌海,2008(05):2+129-130.

[16]　梁嘉.刘三姐歌谣文化的重构与发展[J].广西民族研究,2015(05):106-113.

[17]　刘紫玲.布努瑶创世史诗《密洛陀》[J].民族文学研究,1989(06):32-34.

[18]　龙文波.瑶族长鼓舞的文化阐释[J].吉首大学学报(社会科学版),2009,30(04):150-153.

[19]　卢笛.广西文场起源与流变研究[J].音乐创作,2013,No.263(07):145-147.

[20]　吕瑞荣.毛南族肥套仪式及其文化象征[J].广西民族大学学报(哲学社会科学版),2013,35(01):102-105.

[21]　麦上锋,张晓春.藤县舞狮分类与文化习俗分析[J].广西民族师范学院学报,2013,30(05):41-45.

[22] 宁立正.壮族文化产品的输出及影响——以那坡"黑衣壮"民歌为例[J].广西民族研究,2011(04):94-96.

[23] 农学冠.壮族歌圩的源流[J].广西民族学院学报（社会科学版）,1981(2):37-44.

[24] 潘其旭.壮族歌圩研究[M]. 广西人民出版社, 1991.

[25] 覃乃昌.布洛陀文化体系述论[J].广西民族研究,2003(03):65-72.

[26] 覃乃昌.《嘹歌》:壮族歌谣文化的经典——壮族《嘹歌》文化研究之一[J].广西民族研,2005(01):88-93.

[27] 孙进.从民间传说探寻京族独弦琴产生的文化背景[J].大众文艺,2009(23):91.

[28] 唐元超,蒋东升.白裤瑶"勤泽格拉"丧葬仪式的功能及象征——基于广西南丹县怀里瑶寨的田野调查[J].沈阳大学学报(社会科学版),2019,21(03):372-375.

[29] 田敏,陈文元.论民族关键符号与铸牢中华民族共同体意识——以南宁市三月三民歌节为例[J].云南民族大学学报(哲学社会科学版),2019,36(01):24-30.

[30] 韦鲜.广西马山壮族三声部民歌的音乐特征探究[J].当代音乐,2020(03):63-64.

[31] 韦妙才."跳岭头":傩文化的活化石——桂西南"跳岭头"研究之一[J].钦州学院学报,2010,25(01):33-37.

[32] 魏蓓.作为民族的经典与传统——重读韦其麟的《百鸟衣》[J].广西社

会科学,2020(10):169-173.

[33] 吴霜.凌云壮族七十二巫调的"阴阳"传承[J].民族艺术,2011,No.102(01):124-126.

[34] 谢金娇.新中国"刘三姐"研究70年[J].广西社会科学,2019(12):172-177.

[35] 谢少万,刘小春.瑶族史诗《密洛陀》的民族哲学观[J].广西民族研究,2011(02):123-127.

[36] 许晓明.壮族霜降节:迎霜粽香庆丰稔趁圩歌扬念英雄[J].当代广西,2011(21):57-58.

[37] 许晓明.从族群标识到文化共享——20世纪80年代以来壮族三月三的变迁[J].广西民族师范学院学报,2018,35(06):8-12.

[38] 原媛,翁晔.独具特色的京族乐器——独弦琴[J].今日科苑,2009(14):181.

[39] 杨尚春.广西田阳舞狮运动的发展现状及对策研究[J].百色学院学报,2009,22(05):122-125.

[40] 张秋萍.民俗重塑与海洋文化传承:广西钦州"跳岭头"的播迁与流变——广西传统民俗文化研究之二[J].广西社会科学,2016(11):30-35.

[41] 周华.崇拜种族繁衍的民俗——宾阳舞炮龙运动的社会学考证[J].南京体育学院学报(社会科学版),2009,23(03):54-57.

[42] 周琳.桂林渔鼓音乐的功能价值与保护性传承[J].艺术百家,2013,29(S1):261-262+260.

中国非物质文化遗产网 - 中国非物质文化遗产数字博物馆官网
https://www.ihchina.cn/

广西非物质文化遗产保护网 https://www.gxfybhw.cn/

作者简介

孟繁旭

桂林理工大学外国语学院副教授,博士,硕士生导师。主要从事文化翻译研究和外语教育研究。主持省部级科研项目1项,市厅级2项,参与多项国家级及省部级科研项目。在国内外各类期刊发表学术论文20余篇,出版著作1部。

诸慧琴

韩国全州大学经营学院教授,博士,博士生导师。专业为国际商务,从事中韩翻译和国际商务相关研究。曾参与过韩国国家级及道级科研项目。在国内外各类期刊发表学术论文60余篇,出版著作10部。

非物质文化遗产在广西
Intangible Cultural Heritage in Guangxi
중국 광시의 무형문화유산

2024년 9월 15일 초판 1쇄 인쇄
2024년 9월 20일 초판 1쇄 발행

저　자 | 맹번욱, 제혜금 ◆ 共著

발 행 처 | 도서출판 에듀컨텐츠휴피아
발 행 인 | 李 相 烈
등록번호 | 제2017-000042호 (2002년 1월 9일 신고등록)
주　　소 | 서울 광진구 자양로 28길 98, 동양빌딩
전　　화 | (02) 443-6366
팩　　스 | (02) 443-6376
e-mail　 | iknowledge@naver.com
web　　 | http://cafe.naver.com/eduhuepia
만든사람들 | 기획·김수아 / 책임편집·이진훈 홍문정 정민경 하지수
　　　　　　디자인·유충현 / 영업·이순우

ISBN | 978-89-6356-392-3 (93600)

정　가 | 15,000원

ⓒ 2024, 맹번욱, 제혜금, 도서출판 에듀컨텐츠휴피아

이 책은 저작권법에 따라 보호받는 저작물이므로 무단전재와 무단복제를 금지하며, 책 내용의 전부 또는 일부를 이용하려면 반드시 저작권자 및 도서출판 에듀컨텐츠휴피아의 서면 동의를 받아야 합니다.